International Trade: Traditional Theory, Current Research, and Practical Application

Nicholas Jewczyn

iUniverse, Inc.
New York   Bloomington

International Trade: Traditional Theory,
Current Research, and Practical Application

Copyright © 2010 by Nicholas Jewczyn

iUniverse books may be ordered through booksellers or by contacting:

iUniverse
1663 Liberty Drive
Bloomington, IN 47403
www.iuniverse.com
1-800-Authors (1-800-288-4677)

ISBN: 978-1-4502-0359-3 (sc)
ISBN: 978-1-4502-0360-9 (ebk)

Library of Congress Control Number: 2009944160

Printed in the United States of America

Cover design by Alysa Butterfield

iUniverse rev. date: 1/14/2010

Dedication

This Economics book is dedicated to our 25 pound red tabby, known in and about our community as "Morris." As business cohorts and companions go, Morris was a constant confidante during my six years of insurance agency management, as the assistant to my role as the agency's principal, and he proved to be an excellent "sounding board" as he spent his days sunning himself under the high-intensity lamp in my office. Further, Morris demonstrated a remarkable reserve in his considerable patience with derivatives and portfolio management, through a propitious use of the "Greeks," in manually adjusting the content and value of institutional portfolio models in my M.B.A. program. Finally, Morris became the mascot in my 8000-level, Ph.D., Applied Statistics class and was loved by one and all the students, eventually achieving legendary status in his appellation as the "Stats Cat." It is my considered opinion, based upon the thousands of hours of exposure to financials, econometric models, and business theory, that the Stats Cat will continue to return more to my community's business value than most of the business consultants whom I have met and with whom I have worked (to date).

Abstract

Breadth

The Breadth demonstration will consist of a 30-page scholarly paper that critically assesses the synthesis of international trade thought of the five primary theorists, Isard, Heckscher, Ohlin, Krugman, and Ricardo, concerning international trade. The demonstration will evaluate the strengths and limitations of the tenets of international trade, as espoused by the principal international trade theorists, for the purpose of establishing how their cumulative, theoretical work has contributed to the development of international trade theory. The purpose of this analysis is to establish how their cumulative, theoretical work has contributed to the development of international trade, and to the development of a platform of values that is useful in international trade as it relates to international trade theory, national foreign policy, and the conduct of trade internationally among nations.

Abstract

Depth

The Depth component of this demonstration will be comprised of two parts. The first part will be an annotated bibliography of 15 cited sources (i.e., refereed journal articles written in the past five years) around the Breadth topic objectives. One source is six years old, but is extraordinarily informative and was included for its "classic" status in this survey. The second part of the Depth component will consist of a research literature review essay of some 25 pages on those topic objectives.

Abstract

Application

The Application demonstration project will be comprised of the development of a theoretical, overall structure of a presentation that could be used in a specific application as a briefing symposium for "C-class" corporate officers who will help to conduct international trade on behalf of multi-national corporations. The Application component will also consist of a scholarly essay of about 10 pages and will critically evaluate this theoretical presentation of some 25 pages of slides and notes in light of the theories from the Breadth and the research from the Depth. The contemporary, constructive, social change purpose of this application construct is the prospective enlightenment of corporate "C-class" officers so that these officers are more aware of the constructive choices available for international trade. These officers will then be better informed to effectively conduct such trade, cognizant of some of the current research and protocols, in order to promote global "win-win" trading among nations.

Contents

BREADTH   1

Ricardian Trade Theory   5
   Relative Value and Comparative Advantage   5
   Capital and Rejoinders with Contemporaries   6
   Taxation as Consumption of Capital   7
   Trade bounties   7
   The Mercantile System and Foreign Importation   9
   Trade Exclusivity, Channel Considerations, and
   Globalization   10
   Ricardian Trade Theory Summary   11

Heckscher-Ohlin Trade Theory   14
   Theoretical Positions Concerning H-O Trade Theory
     14
   Heckscher-Ohlin Trade Theory Assumptions   15
   Impediments to Trade and the Use of Trade as a
   Weapon   18
   Ohlin Argued Two Points for Theoretical
   Redemption   19
   A Comparison of the Ricardian and Heckscher-
   Ohlin Trade Theories   20
   Heckscher-Ohlin Trade Theory Summary   21

The Gravity Model of Trade   24
   Introduction   24
   Gravity Model of Trade Explained   25
   Walter Isard, Bertil Ohlin, and the H-O Model   26
   Isard's Intuition Concerning Theory Improvement
     27

A Synthesis of Theoretical Thought   28
Gravity Model of Trade Summary   30

New Trade Theory   32
  Free Trade and New Trade Theory   32
  In Defense of Free Trade   33
  No Adverse Aspects of New Trade Theory   34
  New Trade Theory Summary   35

Breadth Summary   38

DEPTH   41

Annotated Bibliography   43

Literature Review Essay   61
  Introduction   61
  International Trade and the Mechanics of Statecraft   63
  International Trade Structural Linkages in Treaty Negotiations   64
  International Trade Regulation as a Response to Export Discrimination   65
  Intranational and International Adjustments to Liberalized, International Trade   67
  Trade Politics and Foreign Policy in Multi-Lateral International Trade   69
  Trade Liberalization and Economic Growth in Developing Countries   70
  Protectionism, Restrictions, and Barriers to Contemporary International Trade   72
  Mercantilist Commercial Policy and the Regulation of International Trade   73
  Classic, Economic History, Policy Responses to International Trade Challenges   75
  Uses of Economic Statecraft to Foster Secondary State, International Trade Support   77

The Use of U.S. Dollars as the International
Currency for Oil, International Trade   79
The Exercise of the European Union's Trade Power
in International Trade   80
The Five Wars of International Trade Resulting From
the Spread of Globalization   82
Influences on the European Union's External Trade
Policy   83
The Deep Trade Agenda, Trade Politics, and Market
Integration of the European Union   85

Depth Summary   87

APPLICATION   89

Introduction   91

Application Essay   93
Trade Mission Structure and Corporate Performance
        93
Trade Barriers, Capital Flows, Globalization, and
Politics in International Trade   94
International Trade Between Southern States and
Latin America   96
The Decline of National Sovereignty With Relation
to International Trade   97
Implications for International Trade and Integration
Resulting from Globalization   99
Economic Development and Multinational
Corporations   100
Trade Promotion Through the Use of the
International Organization for Standardization   102

Application Summary   104

References   105

APPENDIX 1   111

BREADTH

Theoretical International Trade

Introduction

The Breadth demonstration consists of a scholarly paper that critically assesses the synthesis of international trade thought of the five primary theorists, Isard, Heckscher, Ohlin, Krugman, and Ricardo. This author evaluates the strengths and limitations of the tenets of international trade, as espoused by the principal international trade theorists, for the purpose of establishing how their cumulative, theoretical work has contributed to the development of international trade theory.

The issues that are addressed, concerning Ricardian trade theory, are: relative value and comparative advantage; capital and rejoinders with contemporaries; taxation as consumption of capital; trade bounties; the mercantile system and foreign importation; trade exclusivity, channel considerations, and globalization; and a recapitulation of Ricardian theory. The issues that are addressed, concerning Heckscher-Ohlin trade theory, are: theoretical positions concerning H-O trade theory; Heckscher-Ohlin trade theory assumptions; impediments to trade and the use of trade as a weapon; Ohlin argued two points for theoretical redemption; a comparison of the Ricardian and Heckscher-Ohlin trade theories; a recapitulation of Heckscher-Ohlin trade theory. The issues that are addressed, concerning the gravity model of trade, are: an introduction; the gravity model of trade explained; Walter Isard, Bertil Ohlin, and the H-O model; Isard's intuition concerning theory improvement; a synthesis of theoretical thought; a recapitulation of the gravity model of trade. The issues that are addressed, concerning new trade theory, are: free trade and new trade theory; in defense of free trade; no adverse aspects of new trade theory; a recapitulation of new trade theory.

The purpose of this analysis is to establish how the theorists' cumulative, theoretical work has contributed to the development of international trade, and to the development of a platform of values that was useful in international trade as it related to international trade theory, national foreign policy, and the conduct of trade internationally among nations.

Ricardian Trade Theory

Relative Value and Comparative Advantage

Ricardo ([1817], 2004) postulated some basic rules for trade, whether the trade was conducted domestically, between home provinces, or between nations, and these rules broke out into a number of considerations. One consideration was the fact that location does matter in the conduct of trade. Ricardo noted that rules for the government oversight of the factors of production, with regard to valuation or relative value, between countries were not necessarily the same oversight guidelines used in such oversight domestically; in a particular home country (p. 81). The logical pursuit of the consideration of *relative value,* delineated above, eventually lead interminably to specialization and a further trade consideration. This further trade consideration was described by Ricardo such that, in a free market economy, nations typically allocated the factors of production to the production of trade goods, which economically benefited that particular nation. Further, this unique advantage had a cumulative, beneficial impact on the overall economy domestically, for that nation, and in the world markets of free trade (p. 81). This was the theoretical, foundational statement for the economic, international trade principle more conventionally known as comparative advantage. Each nation pursued, economically, the most opportune production of products and services, which would lead to the lowest cost when exchanged with other traders. The traders from other provinces, or other nations, for the goods and services that would provide an exchange resulting in the merchants' realization of the highest profit margin for such trades, would conclude such transactions with a profitable result for the trading parties concerned (Ricardo [1817], 2004).

Capital and Rejoinders with Contemporaries

Ricardo did occasionally arouse enmity and ire, as reactions from his economist contemporaries, when he chose to respond to various publications, articles, or speeches by those contemporaries that addressed a variety of subjects. This type of interaction had a direct bearing upon his interplay with contemporaries and did influence his theoretical contributions to international trade theory. Ricardo ([1817], 2004) related one such interchange when he mentioned that he had responded to Adam Smith, claiming that Ricardo was less than forthcoming about Ricardo's apparent lack of concern for the human condition of labor. The French economist, Jean-Baptiste Say, had proceeded to assail Ricardo over this rejoinder and Ricardo resoundingly made matters plain that Say had misunderstood the intent and tenor of Ricardo's comments (p. 235). This set the tone for some animosity between Ricardo and Say and Ricardo would continue to disagree with Say on other matters of greater import (Ricardo [1817], 2004). Ricardo maintained that Adam Smith's contention that separate employments of capital in two different countries, parties to a trade, was indeed a fallacy because capital was indeed capital and was doubled to produce goods, whether those goods were eventually intended for local or international resale; the capital on a local level, secondary to production, still required replacement. Ricardo also disagreed with Say's assessment of the proportional allotment of capital, with regard to the trades versus labor, since he had contended that there was not a specific description of the use of such capital allotments actually delineated by Say (p. 236).

Taxation as Consumption of Capital

Some relationships were, between the various types of capital and how those capital types were used to influence trade, part of a discussion concerning the various sorts of production that could eventually result in trade; whether that trade was local, or international in nature. Ricardo ([1817], 2004) noted that capital in general was of a "durable" (p. 94) nature and that the capital of a nation was further broken down into two categories known as "fixed or circulating" (p. 94). Ricardo's policy on capital was certainly frank, when he definitively stated that: it was certainly possible to raise production levels, in order to augment such capital levels; or that it was conversely possible to augment capital levels with the reduction of the consumption of such goods and services, by consumers, in a less frivolous manner from the aggregate economy (p. 94). Ricardo further admonished that taxation did eventually have some relationship to production and thus trade. The government could tax, or a form of government consumption could tax, and thereby reduce capital. So, when higher government taxes were levied and the capital was not augmented by lower public consumption or higher production, Ricardo noted that capital was reduced through consumption, via the mode of taxation, so that the capital available for constructive production would then accordingly be diminished (p. 94).

Trade bounties

The economic consequences and rewards secondary to various types of trade encouragement and restrictions were plain to Ricardo. Ricardo ([1817], 2004) noted that a commodity could not be sold for a higher price domestically than for what it was exported and sold for in another nation's exchanges. However, if a trade supplement, known as a "bounty" (p. 201), were added to the price, then the commodity could then be sold for a considerably lower price abroad and higher prices domestically, because the difference in pricing had been supplemented. Although the domestic price would rise in the short-run, and capital would be withdrawn from manufactures to slide toward the market that paid such a bounty supplement, it would only be a matter of time before equalization occurred. In the long-run, there was a zero-sum effect on natural pricing or on what could be described as the actual production costs. It was simply a manifestation of a short-run effect on the marketplace, and on temporary market prices, which would then automatically rectify themselves (p. 201). Therefore, the domestic price would decrease to what was conventionally known as the needful or more natural price and international markets would then follow suit by adjusting pricing to follow the domestic pricing of the exporter (p. 201). The net result would be that equilibrium would again be reached in the home country for the commodity's price and exportation of the commodity would be subject to the lowest price, and accordingly the lowest profit, at which such a good could still be exported for *any* profit. Thus, with regard to corn, for example, Ricardo noted that bounties on the exports of corn would accordingly lower the price in foreign exchanges, but that there would be no long-term change in the corn pricing domestically (p. 201).

Some considerations arose, pursuant to the use of bounties on exported commodities, which resulted in some additions to trade theory. Ricardo ([1817], 2004) realized that foreign investment, domestically, was encouraged by the enactment of a domestic bounty (p. 212). However, the corollary to that theorem was that, such a bounty, enacted upon the mentioned commodity's export, would indeed decrease the intrinsic value of domestic currency (pp. 211-212). This may not seem to be such a distinction in theory, and the two assertions may even seem to be at odds with one another, with regard to the value attributable to the use of a bounty on exported commodities. Simply explained, the bounties increased the amount of currency that was available domestically, but secondary to the currency increase, pursuant to such bounty trade supplements imposed, the value of the currency, per denomination, was somewhat decreased.

The Mercantile System and Foreign Importation

Ricardo ([1817], 2004) realized that the purpose of the "mercantile system" (p. 212), revealed by Adam Smith, was to enact domestic protectionism, which would result in the higher pricing of domestic commodities on the home country's exchanges, by blocking the import of foreign nations' goods and services (p. 212). Such a system was intent upon moving capital into non-traditional venues where artificial scarcity issues surfaced that created eddies in distribution and consumption so that the use of commodities became skewed. Thus, with this sort of artificial, induced scarcity with some partial or considerable monopolies in manufacturing, production, and distribution, the domestic market could force higher prices since foreign importation was closed and other potential distributors were closed out from the market. Ricardo realized that the long-term, permanent, price increases were maintained by factor of production scarcity and not by increased production shortfalls or manufacturing difficulties (p. 212). Thus, agreeing with Say, Ricardo related that the eventual price, due to the prohibition of foreign importation, was higher domestically but that the higher prices on those affected commodities were not accompanied by higher profits for the merchants or manufacturers who had originally induced their ascendance (Ricardo [1817], 2004).

Ricardo ([1817], 2004) agreed with Adam Smith concerning the observation that the American colonies were somewhat at a disadvantage, with regard to international trade. The colonies did not enjoy a free and open trade to market their manufactures and goods to the open markets of the world, but were aligned with Britain to furnish subsistence commodities at inflated prices while the colonies', produced trade was marketed to the rest of the world at a discount; all the while Britain acting as the benevolent purveyor, who extracted the ripe, financial center from each trade transaction. This enforced commerce treaty, between Britain and her American colonies, was an enforced monopoly for a time. Although the Americans were at first indulgent, the home country that derived so great a benefit, from such an enforced monopoly on the part of her colonies, could not *de facto* continue for very long such a *de jure* arrangement, in light of a continuing array of increasing duties, forever (p. 228).

Trade Exclusivity, Channel Considerations, and Globalization

Ricardo ([1817], 2004) supported Say's position when he noted that higher commodity production costs, even though that commodity under consideration was essential to the economy, or to consumers, would not be a proximal cause to the actual consumption of such a commodity (p. 231). Even though price was derived from production costs, Ricardo disagreed with Say's conclusions that supply and demand regulated pricing. Ricardo conclusively maintained that production does directly influence pricing of commodities and that any sort of competing consumer relationships, or the proportions of supply and demand, were in actuality immaterial (p.231). This became an important aspect of international trade concerning Britain and her American colonies. Ricardo intuitively coupled this intrinsic conclusion, with Adam Smith's assumptions that, since Britain had a monopoly of trade with her American colonies, this sort of exclusive trade with the colonies had fortuitously improved the actual profits taken from the cumulative amount of trade. Essentially, this had occurred because the ability to market goods and services, as inexpensively as other nations, had been reduced (p. 231).

There were a variety of other considerations, not necessarily as a whole, but when taken singly in certain situations, could change the balance of trade; domestically or internationally. Ricardo ([1817], 2004) realized that trade could be affected by: wars that altered the distribution channel for trade or eliminated the availability of a commodity completely (p. 176); new domestic taxes on commodities that could actually destroy an entire nation's comparative advantage for a commodity, service, or product (p. 175); a sudden lack of silver specie to conduct commerce (p. 83); currency movement, secondary to trade transactions between countries, where distinct valuation was altered (pp. 87, 89); and free trade associated with other competing countries, who attempted trading incursions into commercial treaty guaranteed monopolies between international trading partners (pp. 218, 21). It should be noted that Ricardo held a dim view of national government enforced sanctions, which prohibited free trade, and was an early proponent of free trade among all nations, governed by the rules of the marketplace. This ideology placed Ricardo in the unique position of being an early proponent of globalization (p. 213).

Ricardian Trade Theory Summary

Ricardo ([1817], 2004) postulated some basic rules for trade, whether the trade was conducted domestically, between home provinces, or between nations, and these rules broke out into a number of considerations. For example, the same rule which regulated the relative value of commodities in one country did not regulate the relative value of the commodities exchanged between two or more countries. Each nation pursued, economically, the most opportune production of products and services, which would lead to the lowest cost when exchanged with other traders. The traders from other provinces, or other nations, for the goods and services that would provide an exchange resulting in the merchants' realization of the highest profit margin for such trades, would conclude such transactions with a profitable result for the trading parties concerned (Ricardo [1817], 2004).

Ricardo ([1817], 2004) related one such interchange, when he mentioned that he had responded to Adam Smith, claiming that he was less than forthcoming about Ricardo's apparent lack of concern for the human condition of labor. Ricardo's policy on capital was certainly frank, when he definitively stated that, capital may therefore be increased by an increased production, or by a diminished unproductive consumption. Ricardo ([1817], 2004) noted that a commodity could not be sold for a higher price domestically, than for what it was exported and sold for in another nation's exchanges.

However, if a trade supplement, known as a bounty, were added to the price, then the commodity could then be sold for a considerably lower price abroad and higher prices domestically, because the difference in pricing had been supplemented. Although the domestic price would rise in the short-run, and capital would be withdrawn from manufactures to slide toward the market that paid such a bounty supplement, it would only be a matter of time before equalization occurred. The causes, which would operate on the market price, would produce no effect whatever on its natural price, or its real cost of production. Therefore, the domestic price would decrease to the natural and necessary price and the foreign market would also lower its price in the country to which it was exported. The net result would be that equilibrium would again be reached in the home country for the commodity's price and exportation of the commodity would be subject to the lowest price, and accordingly the lowest profit, at which such a good could still be exported for any profit. Such a system was intent upon moving capital into non-traditional venues where artificial scarcity issues surfaced that created eddies in distribution and consumption so that the use of commodities became skewed.

The colonies did not enjoy a free and open trade to market their manufactures and goods to the open markets of the world, but were aligned with Britain to furnish subsistence commodities at inflated prices while the colonies', produced trade was marketed to the rest of the world at a discount. Britain acted as the benevolent purveyor, to market the colonies' goods and services, and as compensation extracted the ripe, financial center from each trade transaction. This enforced commerce treaty, between Britain and her American colonies, was an enforced monopoly for only a time.

Heckscher-Ohlin Trade Theory

Theoretical Positions Concerning H-O Trade Theory

Isard (1956) noted that trade existed for a variety of reasons. As population centers emerged within nation-states, those emergent population sites were characterized by increased agricultural demand, which then created zones for such demand at each population site (p. 17). This inevitably caused population site patterns that, proximal to the population centers, then lead to increased and improved trade within and without that particular geographic area (p. 17). Ricardo ([1817], 2004) presumed this outcome and Ricardian trade theory was characterized by only one factor of production that could inevitably vary, and this factor was labor productivity. Thus, Ricardian trade theory recognized that a variance in labor productivity would precipitate comparative advantage as an eventual result. So, labor productivity, for a region or nation, would differentiate such an area from other areas occupied by potential trade partners (pp. 104-105). Heckscher and Ohlin ([1919], [1924], 1991) realized that factor proportions were integral to trade theory and that the factors and their proportions were considerably more involved than the single labor factor espoused by Ricardian trade theory

(p. 54). Thus, when a condition of *no trade* changes, such as when factor equivalence was violated, this change then invoked trade according to the tenets of the Heckscher-Ohlin trade theory (Krugman and Obstfeld, 2006). Krugman and Obstfeld (2006) explained that Heckscher-Ohlin trade theory has for decades been critical to, and imperative for, a thorough comprehension of trade results (p. 76). Factor proportions change precipitated the use of the Heckscher-Ohlin trade theory; in practice. The principal objection to H-O theory, that production factors were proportionate, or the Leontief paradox (p. 72), supposedly disavowed H-O theory. This dichotomy would apparently seem to remarkably devalue H-O theory as being even slightly useful to international trade. This troubling dichotomy, and the tenets of H-O theory, will be the subject of discussion throughout the following part of this paper.

Heckscher-Ohlin Trade Theory Assumptions

In order to more completely interweave the more intricate parts of H-O trade theory, Isard (1956) mentioned that it was important to look at the premises of the various theories of international trade. A discussion of the assumptions that provided a platform for H-O theory more adequately confirmed Bertil Ohlin's critical assessment of this trade problem (p. 208). Incidentally, Heckscher and Ohlin had a most interesting and tenuous mentor-mentee, *love-hate* relationship over a period of several decades that did have an effect upon how their combined trade theory evolved over time. Heckscher and Ohlin ([1919], [1924], 1991) noted that Heckscher realized on several occasions that Ohlin was correct, concerning parts of the theory, and had greater respect for Ohlin's abilities (p. 4). However, Ohlin was usually not as generous to Heckscher, his mentor, and noted these perceived shortcomings in print and through lectures (p. 5).

Heckscher and Ohlin ([1919], [1924], 1991) stated that the conventional H-O theory "2x2x2 model" was not found in the original 1919 or the 1924 works, which were both reprinted in the 1991 reprint, in their entirety, along with an introduction from minor theorists who later amended H-O theory. When combined with their later writings in that reprint, the bases for that model were indeed found in the original writings and crystallized in the reprint (p. 25). There were a variety of about one-dozen assumptions that ameliorated the considerations of H-O theory that mathematically and theoretically smoothed the way in which it functioned, on a more practical level. H-O theory made a variety of assumptions. a) Heckscher and Ohlin realized in their model that there were only two nations extant with only two commodities and that only two factors of production were employed, which were labor and capital (p. 6). b) Ohlin ([1933], 1952) noted that the production technology of both nations was indeed the same with his realization that Germany, the U.S., and other nations had all attained virtually the same technological plateau, as mutually developed nations (p. 126). c) For both nations in the model, Heckscher and Ohlin ([1919], [1924], 1991) noted that each nation marketed two commodities, one capital-based and one labor-based, with the example that expressed the understanding that land-based product exports would have the reasonable expectation of being traded for labor-based product imports (p.58).

d) Heckscher and Ohlin ([1919], [1924], 1991) naturally assumed that production would proceed based upon scaled returns that were incessant (p. 26). e) Ohlin ([1933], 1952) completed the eventual logic train of the theoretical assertion, that both nations possessed productive capabilities that were not fully specialized, with the observation that there was surplus, unused, productive capacity wherein average costs were higher than marginal costs (p. 286). f) Ohlin explained that the two nations' tastes were virtually the same with the observation that trade data, taken from customs tallies, noted that both of the nations in the example exported and imported the identical commodities under consideration (p. 96). g) Heckscher and Ohlin ([1919], [1924], 1991) engaged in convoluted and circuitous discussions, in their individual portions of the overall text, about both nations of the model being possessed of factor and commodity markets that exhibited perfect competition, but the most direct route was the discussion about all of these thoughts that also tied in proportional production related to "harmonic equilibrium" (p. 59). h) Ohlin ([1933], 1952) perceived that all interregional trade was a function of the intrinsic nature secondary to the use of the factors of production; that such factors were indeed inseparable (p. 58), and that trade itself was a direct by-product of the fact that those factors were indeed inseparable - those factors were distributed in a lop-sided manner (p. 58). Ohlin concluded, regardless of the underlying cause, that interregional trade was simply the result of the substitution for factors of production that were geographically immobile (p. 58). Further, Ohlin addressed the divisibility and international mobility issues with finality when he stated that the only areas of significance, in this regard, were sovereign countries, which was the main rationale for addressing this issue through the discussion concerning international trade (p. 52). To conclude, these platform planks meant that there was not factor mobility on the international scene, but that there was perfect factor mobility domestically.

i) Heckscher and Ohlin ([1919], [1924], 1991) concluded, in the H-O model, that there were no impediments whatsoever to international trade, resulting from any issues associated with examples of conceivable drawbacks, such as possible bounties, sanctions, embargoes, or tariffs. Further, it was logical to assume that all goods were considered to be traded goods, since there was a complete lack of costs associated with the transport of such goods (p. 22). j) Heckscher and Ohlin ([1919], [1924], 1991) decided that there was a direct, proportional relationship between the imported goods of one country and the exported goods of another country, since it was assumed that, in both countries concerned, the production factors were exactly liberated in direct proportions from one country to the next (p. 50). Since this was the assumed case, trade on the international markets would result in zero net changes to the production factor scarcity in the nation that performed the product importation (p. 50). When these two points coincided and held true in trade, then it followed that, for both nations in the H-O model, there must have been full utilization of all resources in both nations. k) To conclude the assumptions set of the H-O model, the capstone thought of both nations of the model, having had a completely balanced, international trade, in isolation, was suggested by the extreme condition that, in light of no capital movement internationally, the trade balances between the hypothetical nations would exhibit equilibrium (p. 125).

Impediments to Trade and the Use of Trade as a Weapon

There were types of impediments to trade, natural and unnatural, and these had variegated impacts upon the practical tenets espoused by H-O trade theory. Heckscher and Ohlin ([1919], [1924], 1991) explained that tariffs, and other barriers to trade, competed with the natural tendency for international trade to compensate for the scarcity of the factors of production between nations (p. 185). Although the theory itself disavowed such activity, in the theoretical world, the theorists would have been remiss not to at least address in passing such tenuous, international circumstances in international trade. It was politically expedient of both Heckscher and Ohlin to point out a practical solution for circumventing the various issues associated with tariffs by noting that import tariffs decreased the ease with which a nation could export goods and services.

The nation concerned was then obliged to prompt domestic companies to create subsidiaries in those foreign countries to reduce such protectionist tendencies (p. 185). This became the theoretical basis for the contemporary creation of multi-national corporations.

Building upon the introduced platforms of the previous two trade theories presented in this paper, oblique references will begin to intercede on behalf of the original impetus behind this paper: the use of international trade as an implement of national, foreign policy. Heckscher (1922) pointed out, with a little economic, historical flourish, that even Louis had personally observed considerable British trade wares adorning the shops in Leyden, Holland. Since the Napoleonic Wars were in progress at the time under discussion, Napoleon was incensed at the Dutch for helping Britain through the purchase of her trade goods, the proceeds of which would be used to carry on the war with Napoleon. After Napoleon had issued his September 16, 1808 decree, effectively closing French borders to all Dutch trade goods, as his national foreign policy response with the use of international trade as a weapon, the Dutch responded in kind. On October 23, 1808, the Dutch responded with the extraordinarily strict policy that closed all ports. Not only were exports completely prohibited, but also all vessels, foreign and domestic, would be summarily attacked when they entered any Dutch harbor (p. 178).

Ohlin Argued Two Points for Theoretical Redemption

In reflection upon the body of theoretical thought involving trade theory in general, Ohlin ([1933], 1952) made certain that two points were brought to the fore in order to redeem H-O trade theory in general and his reputation among the brethren of the economist academic clique in particular. He criticized Bastable for comments concerning capital movements between nations (p. 589) when it was, even at that time, clear that trade theory orthodoxy dictated the universally accepted conclusion that labor and capital simply did not move back and forth between nations (p. 589). The second point was simply that there was becoming, of late, too great of an emphasis on variations in wages and an over-riding exclusion of additional capital income, when global trade structure was discussed with relation to the limited movement of capital and trade variations (p. 589).

A Comparison of the Ricardian and Heckscher-Ohlin Trade Theories

Krugman and Obstfeld (2006) concluded that any one model might not be completely descriptive of the situations involving international trade and that it would be more appropriate and valuable to use a combination of trade models to examine actual trade problems (p. 84). Thus, these theorists noted that in order to effectively investigate issues resulting from accelerated growth of production, it was appropriate to employ the Ricardian model for examination (p. 84). However, for a different set of circumstances, perhaps if we desired to examine American distribution of income, secondary to the results from improved trade, the H-O model would be more appropriate (p. 84). The authors concluded that the models were in actuality particular cases of the over-arching, general model of the economics of world trade and they compared the Ricardian and H-O models with the following observations:

1.   The productive capacity of an economy can be summarized by its production possibility frontier, and differences in these frontiers give rise to trade.

2.   Production possibilities determine a country's relative supply schedule.

3.   World equilibrium is determined by world relative demand and a *world* relative supply schedule that lies between the national relative supply schedules. (p. 84)

Heckscher-Ohlin Trade Theory Summary

Isard (1956) noted that trade existed for a variety of reasons. Ricardo ([1817], 2004) presumed that and Ricardian trade theory was characterized by only one factor of production that could inevitably vary; this factor was labor productivity. Heckscher and Ohlin ([1919], [1924], 1991) realized that factor proportions were integral to trade theory and that the factors and their proportions were considerably more involved than the single labor factor espoused by Ricardian trade theory. In order to more completely interweave the more intricate parts of H-O trade theory, Isard (1956) mentioned that it was important to look at the premises of the various theories of international trade and a discussion of the assumptions that provided a platform for H-O theory was in order to more adequately discuss Ohlin's excellent formulation of the problem.

Heckscher and Ohlin had a most interesting and tenuous mentor-mentee, love-hate relationship over a period of several decades characterized by the Heckscher and Ohlin ([1919], [1924], 1991) comments of how Heckscher must have realized that Ohlin was right about a number of aspects of the H-O model; his respect for Ohlin grew over time as opposed to the fact that Ohlin was considerably less generous to Heckscher in print and in lectures.

Heckscher and Ohlin ([1919], [1924], 1991) stated that the conventional H-O theory 2x2x2 model was not found in the original 1919 or the 1924 works, which were both reprinted in the 1991 reprint in their entirety along with an introduction from minor theorists who later amended H-O theory, but when combined with their later writings in the reprint, the bases for that model were indeed found in the original writings and crystallized in the reprint.

There were a variety of about one-dozen assumptions that ameliorated the considerations of H-O theory that mathematically and theoretically smoothed the way in which it functioned on a more practical level. H-O theory made a variety of assumptions. Heckscher and Ohlin realized in their model that there were only two nations extant with only two commodities and that only two factors of production were employed, which were labor and capital. Ohlin ([1933], 1952) noted that the production technology of both nations was indeed the same. Heckscher and Ohlin ([1919], [1924], 1991) assumed constant returns to scale. Ohlin ([1933], 1952) completed the eventual logic train of the theoretical assertion that both nations possessed productive capabilities that were not fully specialized. Production capacity was so little utilized that marginal costs fell below the level of average costs. So, it subsequently followed that all interregional trade, whether due to the one cause or the other, might be regarded as a substitute for the lack of geographical mobility of the productive factors. Further, in this event, international trade would result in no change whatsoever in the relative scarcity of the factors of production in the importing country.

Heckscher and Ohlin ([1919], [1924], 1991) explained that, like all trade barriers, tariffs acted primarily to counteract the tendency of trade to bring about interregional equalization of factor scarcity. Although the theory itself disavowed such activity in the theoretical world, the authors would have been remiss not to at least address in passing such tenuous, international circumstances in international trade. Building upon the introduced platforms of the previous two trade theories presented in this paper, oblique references were made to intercede on behalf of the original impetus behind this paper: the use of international trade as an implement of national, foreign policy. Since the Napoleonic Wars were in progress at the time, for this example, Napoleon was incensed at the Dutch for helping Britain through the purchase of her trade goods, the proceeds of which would be used to carry on the war with Napoleon. After Napoleon had issued his September 16, 1808 decree, effectively closing French borders to all Dutch trade goods, as his national foreign policy response with the use of international trade as a weapon, the Dutch responded in kind.

In reflection upon the body of theoretical thought involving trade theory in general, Ohlin ([1933], 1952) made certain that two points were brought to the fore, in order to redeem H-O trade theory in general, and his reputation among the brethren of the economist academic clique in particular.

Krugman and Obstfeld (2006) concluded that any one model might not be completely descriptive of the situations involving international trade, and that it would be more appropriate and valuable, when we analyze real problems, to base our insights on a mixture of the various models. Thus, these authors noted that in order to effectively investigate issues resulting from rapid productivity growth, we may want to apply the Ricardian model. The possibility frontier, and differences in these frontiers gave rise to trade. The Ricardian and H-O theories compared:

1. The productive capacity of an economy can be summarized by its production possibility frontier, and differences in these frontiers give rise to trade.
2. Production possibilities determine a country's relative supply schedule.
3. World equilibrium is determined by world relative demand and a *world* relative supply schedule that lies between the national relative supply schedules.

The Gravity Model of Trade

Introduction

Krugman and Obstfeld (2006) maintained that the gravity model of trade explained the trade value between two nations, expounded upon difficulties that hampered the conduct of global trade, and was a direct, raw data relationship concerning international trade (p. 10). Helpman and Krugman (1985) realized some advanced concepts related to the conduct of international trade in general and the gravity model in particular. After considerable mathematical derivation and intuition, these authors concluded that if nations that were industrialized were to retain a certain status or size, proportional to the global economy, then the nations' trade amounts would grow increasingly faster when the relational group's size, of developed nations, leveled with respect to the passage of time (p. 167). Many financiers who move capital internationally, nation-state policy formulators, and econometrics tabulators the world over were probably wondering what this observation had to do with the propagation and maintenance of international trade, with relationship to the previously mentioned gravity model? Fortunately, the authors were able to answer this hypothetical question in kind and they irrefutably tied the two concepts together in their postulated, theoretical conclusions. The authors surmised that scaled economies fostered the specialization that did not usually appear in the more conventional world of constant returns, so the gravity model's mathematics were a better description of patterns of international trade (p. 167).

Gravity Model of Trade Explained

There were questions left unanswered, however, about the specific nature of the gravity model and how the calculations were empirically derived in order to make such a model of international trade useful. Krugman and Obstfeld (2006) explained a number of concepts associated with the gravity model with:

> Looking at world trade as a whole, economists have found that an equation of the following form predicts the volume of trade between any two countries fairly accurately,
>
> $$Tij = A \times Y_i \times Yj/Dij,$$
>
> $$(2\text{-}1)$$
>
> where A is a constant term, Tij is the value of trade between country i and country j, Y_i is country $i's$ GDP, Yj is country $j's$ GDP, and Dij is the distance between the two countries. That is, the value of trade between any two countries is proportional, other things equal, to the *product* of the two countries' GDPs, and diminishes with the distance between the two countries. (p. 12)

The mathematical model shown above, which was a relatively obvious off-shoot and common-knowledge reference to the classical, Newtonian, gravitational law, provided a basic platform that a number of theorists, over the years, have been able to use to either accept or refute the gravity model of trade (p. 17). In order to effectively handle all of the increased input into the various types of models used for the evaluation of international trade, Isard ([1956], 1972) discussed in detail his work, in the use of a variety of models, including the gravity model of trade, that was of use in the estimation of the elements associated with interregional models of such trade (p. 287).

Walter Isard, Bertil Ohlin, and the H-O Model

Isard ([1956], 1972) made some interesting observations of the general trade theory, more commonly known as the Heckscher-Ohlin trade theory, when he discussed a variety of elements secondary to the theory and some interrelationships concerning dogma considerations and various opinions or criticisms. It was plain that Isard held H-O theory in relatively low esteem, when he indicated that he understood H-O theory to be only a sort of spoken, timid, general sort of attainment of locality considerations. Isard continued to downplay the general trade H-O model, not even having observed that Heckscher had made some foundational contributions to it, with discussions concerning the fact that costing, with regard to a particular sector of a region, was not uniform; a theoretical plank purportly proposed by Ohlin in the H-O model. Further, Isard mentioned that the theory wavered in and out from the intended theoretical platform entirely. He ravaged Ohlin with comments concerning Ohlin's lack of astute generalizations and parallels, intimating that Ohlin was never able to create a uniform general theory that would bridge the theoretical chasm between the localization of productive factors and the intrinsic consumer interests along with any sort of international theory of trade. Isard humiliated Ohlin further with statements such as the fact that, in a number of instances, the general trade theory, descriptive of the H-O model, was abandoned entirely in favor of something that was patently and theoretically workable, such as "typical Weberian style" (p. 52). This sort of intrigue and abject humiliation did not exist in a vacuum, and it certainly was not isolated, since Isard contended that Losch had also condemned Ohlin's lack of a certain response to the regional location issues, and with the persistent failure to comprehend the fact that labor movements and relationships were secondary to actions in the aggregate economy (p. 53).

Isard ([1956], 1972) noted that Weber was not enthralled with general trade theory, in the classical sense, since the general theory of trade ignored the consideration of the costing associated with the factors of production and finished, piece goods. Isard noted that other theorists had done considerable, theoretical work on the localization theory. Isard did mention that Ohlin, in an apparently rare, conciliatory measure for Isard, had done some noteworthy work on the general trade theory through Ohlin's formulation of a section of localization theory. However, Isard mentioned that this was basically secondary to many other theorists' work on general trade theory and that despite considerable work by Ohlin, and other more stout trade theorists, although minor improvements were realized in the general theory, that trade and location theories would still not be acceptable for practical use (p. 208).

Isard's Intuition Concerning Theory Improvement

Walter Isard was never short on suggestions for the improvement of other published work. Isard ([1956], 1972) grappled with many suggestions for the actual improvement of trade theory, so that it would become more practical and applicable to contemporary situations in international trade. Isard discounted the customary assumption of H-O theory that summarily dismissed the concept of transportation costs eventually entering the chain calculations, to compute trade valuation. Isard noted that the transportation issue was in fact significant and that it did indeed affect the nature and nurture of trade because, relating to distance, locality, and the factors of production in concert with commodities, these accumulated costs could at once become extremely significant. He continued to gravitate toward the locality contributions of Weber, and discounted Ohlin with vague references to Ohlin's lack of intuition of the problem, which could only be expressed *in terms of Weberian dogma*. Isard realized that the costing associated with transportation, which was applied directly to the 2x2x2 theoretical concept of the H-O model, a basic assumption consideration of H-O trade theory, was essentially a function of opportunity cost. Also, that it was directly related to commodity locality with relation to production factors in *both* nations of the H-O model (p. 217).

A Synthesis of Theoretical Thought

Sometimes, what had been neglected to be mentioned or said, could be far more important than what *was* said or mentioned. With regard to a higher level analysis or synthesis of the Isard gravity model of trade with original trade theory - this will not be a function of this paper. For a variety of reasons, which were not made clear by the theorist, it was as though the Ricardian trade theory had never existed; no mention of the Ricardian theory of trade was made by Isard at any juncture in his work. Further, Isard felt the need to, at first, completely discount the general trade theory from the outset. In fact, during the first twenty-four pages of his text, Isard made it a point to start out with descriptions of basic trade theory, as though there had never been any trade theory previously in existence, taking the reader from the concept of fertile ground being over-run by natives, to complicated city-states. These regions then carried on sophisticated trade routes and traded a cornucopia of goods, the trade of which was characterized by all sorts of commercial treaties and interregional agreements (Isard [1956], 1972).

Isard ([1956], 1972) noted that the gravity model had some predictive value for the back and forth flow of international trade between nations. This theorist was able to demonstrate that there were spatial relationships between the sizes, economically, of two nations and the considerations of distance between the trading nations with regard to their actual spatial relationships geographically. So, the gravity model had a lot to do with the spatial relationship template associated with international trade between nations; the flows of goods and commodities to and fro predicated upon the nations' economic size, distances from one another, and the geographical relationships concurrently involved between those nations (p. 281-282). The H-O model, however, predicted the template of trade flows with relation to the advantages of each nation involved, with respect to advantages, comparative or otherwise, related to factors of production. For example, if a certain nation had a surplus of a particular factor of production for some piece goods, it would be logically assumed that the factor in surplus would be increasingly utilized to produce greater amounts of trade goods for export, associated with such a factor (pp. 127-128, 172, 51-52, 208, 217). The Leontief paradox disagreed with this assumption, since the United States, the factor abundant trading nation in contemporary international trade, had actually provided more goods to nations that were viewed as factor abundant, with regard to labor and had shown considerable promise as an analytic tool (pp. 209, 49).

Krugman and Obstfeld (2006) referred to the Linder hypothesis in an oblique manner, with regard to "preferential trading agreements," and noted that nations would pursue a trade pattern template that would reflect the total consumer preferences for such trade goods within a nation where importing was occurring. However, these authors did not credit Staffan Linder by name (pp. 232-233). Helpman and Krugman (1985) noted in an oblique way, not mentioning H-O theory in particular, that the foundations of national, comparative advantage did not necessarily forecast the gravity model's interrelationships within international trade. Even though a nation might compare with another, in international trade, with regard to GDP, there could be an increased, unexplained incidence of international trade. The authors had some reservations concerning the H-O model, and its applicability to international trading scenarios, with relation to the previous example, since some nations with comparable GDPs demonstrated increased trading in non-homogeneous goods, because of like and type values (p. 261).

Gravity Model of Trade Summary

Krugman and Obstfeld (2006) explained that, an empirical relationship known as the gravity model helped to make sense of the value of trade between any pair of countries and also shed some light on the impediments that continued to limit international trade. After considerable mathematical derivation and intuition, these authors concluded that if nations that were industrialized were to maintain an approximately fixed relative size in the world economy, then the within group volume of trade would grow faster than the group's income if and only if the relative size of the industrial countries was equalized over time.

In order to effectively handle all of the increased input into the various types of models used for the evaluation of international trade, Isard ([1956], 1972) discussed in detail his work in the use of a variety of models, including the gravity model of trade, that was of use in the estimation of the elements associated with interregional models of such trade. Isard ([1956], 1972) made some interesting observations of the general trade theory, more commonly known as the Heckscher-Ohlin trade theory, when he discussed a variety of elements secondary to the theory and some interrelationships concerning dogma considerations and various opinions or criticisms.

It was plain that Isard held H-O theory in relatively low esteem, when he indicated that he understood H-O theory to be only a sort of spoken, timid, general sort of attainment of locality considerations. He ravaged Ohlin with comments concerning Ohlin's lack of astute generalizations and parallels, intimating that Ohlin was never able to create a uniform general theory that would bridge the theoretical chasm between the localization of productive factors and consumer interests along with any sort of international theory of trade.

Isard ([1956], 1972) noted that other economists were not enthralled with general trade theory, in the classical sense, since the general theory of trade ignored the consideration of the costing associated with the factors of production and finished, piece goods. Isard noted that other theorists had done considerable, theoretical work on the localization theory. For a variety of reasons, which were not made clear by the theorist, it was as though the Ricardian trade theory had never existed; no mention of the Ricardian theory of trade was made by Isard at any juncture in his work.

Isard was able to demonstrate that there were spatial relationships between the sizes, economically, of two nations and the considerations of distance between the trading nations with regard to their actual spatial relationships geographically. So, the gravity model had a lot to do with the spatial relationship template associated with international trade between nations; the flows of goods and commodities to and fro predicated upon the nations' economic size, distances from one another, and the geographical relationships concurrently involved between those nations.

Helpman and Krugman (1985) noted in an oblique way, not mentioning H-O theory in particular, that the foundations of national, comparative advantage did not necessarily forecast the gravity model's interrelationships within international trade. Even though a nation might compare with another, in international trade, with regard to GDP, there could be an increased, unexplained incidence of trade.

New Trade Theory

Free Trade and New Trade Theory

Heckscher (1922) discussed some aspects of free trade concerning this concept as a precursor to what was at the time known as the continental system. However, this *free ships make free goods* (p. 36) ideology was mainly depicted in the economic history annals as a reference made with regard to aggressive nations, in time of war, turning their trade goods over to the neutral countries for trans-shipment to coastal communities for the journey inland (to market). For example, after a treaty with the infant nation the United States, the emperor Napoleon was politically transfigured to become the staunchest supporter of free trade on the open seas, but this was a belief in name only and the actual status in practice was changed before the ink was even dry on his treaties. This sort of gaming policy, with regard to trade that was free (or otherwise), had come to a swift and sudden conclusion with the Treaty of Amiens in the spring of 1802 (pp. 78-79). Although some would contend that the advent of new trade theory was designed to be a critical rebuttal of the *new idea* of free trade, such new trade theory came into existence with some discussion associated with Helpman and Krugman (1985) and, the notion of free trade as a concept, had already been extant previous to the advent of the nineteenth century (Heckscher, 1922).

In Defense of Free Trade

Krugman and Obstfeld (2006) were proponents of free trade, with their notions that there were ideally two reasons for the actual defense of the concept of free trade: a) a nation's shortcomings, in the domestic market, should be addressed by domestic policies that treated the problem's origins; and, b) since market failure was not well forecasted by economists, those economists should not create those policies (p. 216). The general ideology behind this defense was that market failures should not require a change in international trade policy and that product subsidies should be the rule, instead of the exception, in order to not use measures such as tariffs; measures that would not cause a decrease in the consumption of such products. This was also a veiled argument for the subsidy of fledgling industries that would later come to dominate the world marketplace (Krugman and Obstfeld, 2006). The authors were also not in favor of the congressional subsidy of the automotive industry, but they were less in favor of quotas on imports, since there would be concomitant employment improvements for the aggregate economy. However, the import quotas would eventually change the mechanism of choice for consumers (p. 217).

Krugman and Obstfeld (2006) had realized that, although it might be advantageous for a sovereign nation to adjust their international trade participation, the actual results would be distorted by the nation's own domestic special interest groups that would then thwart the ideology of equilibrium attainment, in the marketplace, in order to realize special interest group goals. The authors were adept at summarizing the over-riding opinion of economists in general with: a) movement away from free trade, in an economy, could imply large costs associated with such movement; b) there were invisible advantages to free trade that increased the costs associated with domestic protectionism; and c) the political mechanism, domestically, would deflect any articulated free trade structural change (p. 210). Thus, although economists could occasionally demonstrate, via a theoretical model, that a variety of international trade sanctions could alter the pattern, value, and volume of free trade, those policies in the actual environment, of the international trading marketplace, were eventually thwarted by forces that operated on the political nation-state's government that then de-stabilized the arena and disallowed market equilibrium in the long run (Krugman and Obstfeld, 2006).

No Adverse Aspects of New Trade Theory

Helpman and Krugman (1985) explained that the there was some synthesis of thought derived from an overview of the different theories, but that there may not be the solution derived that the financiers and economists were actually expecting. With regard to the structure of international trade, the authors realized that levels of production peculiarities supported Ricardian theory and production factor distribution supported the Heckscher-Ohlin theory (pp. 55-56). However, to contrast these views, the authors noted that increasing returns to scale do have a unique effect on the structure of international trade. The authors also noted that, in the presence of economies of scale in nations that do not differ substantially from one another, trade that was vibrant existed and could flourish. They did disagree with certain aspects of Ricardian trade theory, but supported the H-O general model of trade in most situations in international trade for the prediction of trade flows concerning sector endowments. However, the disagreement with Ricardian theory seemed to stem from the notion that comparative advantage did not exist forever, and that there was actually more involved, and at stake in international trade, than just the simplistic notion of the variability of the productivity of labor issue promulgated by the Ricardians (Helpman and Krugman, 1985).

Although Helpman and Krugman (1985) mentioned that the overall concept of increasing returns was integral to international trade, this was no longer the primary reason for such trade and that there were a number of other factors secondary to the considerations of commodities, regulations, factors, and even the productive technologies associated with such products, in international trade. So, perhaps new trade theory was not as much an indictment of the protectionism associated with fledgling or troubled products and markets, or the Ricardian trade theory in general, as perhaps it was more the advent of a more ritualistic and rigorous method of mathematically examining a variety of factors associated with free trade. Although it was not an indictment of international free trade or perhaps even a valid improvement of Ricardian or the H-O model of general trade theory, there just didn't seem to be much that was *new*, about new trade theory. A notable exception to that assertion would be an allowance for some involved mathematics for the actual calculations associated with trade patterns and factor pricing associated with increasing returns to scale, concerning the domestic comparative advantage that a nation-state uses to reach out into the international marketplace (pp. 261-262).

New Trade Theory Summary

Heckscher (1922) discussed some aspects of free trade concerning this concept as a precursor to what was at the time known as the continental system. However, the free ships make free goods ideology was mainly depicted in the economic history annals as a reference made with regard to aggressive nations, in time of war, turning their trade goods over to the neutral countries for trans-shipment to coastal communities for the journey to market. This sort of gaming policy, with regard to trade that was free, or otherwise, had come to a swift and sudden conclusion with the Peace Treaty of Amiens in March of 1802. So, although some would contend that the advent of new trade theory was designed to be a critical rebuttal of the *'new idea'* of free trade, such new trade theory had come into existence with some discussion associated with Helpman and Krugman (1985) and the notion of free trade, as a concept, had already been extant previous to the advent of the nineteenth century (Heckscher, 1922).

The general ideology behind this defense was that market failures should not require a change in international trade policy and that product subsidies should be the rule, instead of the exception, in order to not use measures such as tariffs; measures, such as those sanctions, that would not cause a decrease in the consumption of such products. This was also a veiled argument for the subsidy of fledgling industries that would later come to dominate the world marketplace due to original, domestic protectionism (Krugman and Obstfeld, 2006).

The authors were also not in favor of the American congressional subsidy of the automotive industry, but they were less in favor of quotas on imports since there would be concomitant employment improvements for the aggregate economy, but the import quotas would distort consumer choices that would then alter market-share. Krugman and Obstfeld (2006) had realized that, although it might be advantageous for a sovereign nation to adjust their international trade participation, the actual results would be distorted by their own domestic special interest groups that would then thwart the ideology of equilibrium attainment in the marketplace in order to realize special interest group goals.

Helpman and Krugman (1985) explained that the there was some synthesis of thought derived from an overview of the different theories, but that there may not be the solution derived that financiers and economists were actually expecting.

With regard to the structure of international trade, the authors realized that Ricardian trade theory relied upon differences in the sectoral ranking of relative productivity levels, and the Heckscher-Ohlin trade theory relied upon differences in the composition of factor endowments. However, to contrast these views, the authors noted that increasing returns to scale do have a unique effect on the structure of international trade.

Breadth Summary

The Breadth demonstration consisted of a scholarly paper that critically assessed the synthesis of international trade thought of the five primary theorists, Isard, Heckscher, Ohlin, Krugman, and Ricardo. This author evaluated the strengths and limitations of the tenets of international trade, as espoused by the principal international trade theorists for the purpose of establishing how their cumulative, theoretical work has contributed to the development of international trade theory.

The issues that were addressed concerning Ricardian trade theory were: relative value and comparative advantage; capital and rejoinders with contemporaries; taxation as consumption of capital; trade bounties; the mercantile system and foreign importation; trade exclusivity, channel considerations, and globalization; and a recapitulation of Ricardian theory. The issues that were addressed concerning Heckscher-Ohlin trade theory were: theoretical positions concerning H-O trade theory; Heckscher-Ohlin trade theory assumptions; impediments to trade and the use of trade as a weapon; Ohlin argued two points for theoretical redemption; a comparison of the Ricardian and Heckscher-Ohlin trade theories; and a recapitulation of Heckscher-Ohlin trade theory. The issues that were addressed concerning the gravity model of trade were: an introduction; the gravity model of trade explained; Walter Isard, Bertil Ohlin, and the H-O model; Isard's intuition concerning theory improvement; a synthesis of theoretical thought; and a recapitulation of the gravity model of trade. The issues that were addressed concerning new trade theory were: free trade and new trade theory; in defense of free trade; no adverse aspects of new trade theory; and a recapitulation of new trade theory.

The purpose of this analysis was to establish how the theorists' cumulative, theoretical work has contributed to the development of international trade, and to the development of a platform of values that was useful in international trade as it related to international trade theory, national foreign policy, and the conduct of trade internationally among nations.

DEPTH

Current Research In International Trade

Annotated Bibliography

Afilalo, A. & Patterson, D. (2006). Statecraft, trade and the order of states. *Chicago Journal of International Law*, *6*(2), 725-759. Retrieved January 8, 2009, from Research Library database. (Document ID: 1011292111).

Afilalo and Patterson (2006) composed a period piece that was at once, a theoretical synthesis of the international law pertaining to international trade, and a literature review of international trade in general. However, this was not a study of international trade, *per se*. The synthesis of this article was provided in three general parts: a discussion of the evolution of international trading states in the twentieth-century, after World War Two, concerning strategy and statesmanship; the organizational nature of the relationships between statecraft and international trade, with relation to the structural links associated with such issues; and the relationships between the various pieces of legislation and treaties, such as the General Agreement on Tariffs and Trade (GATT) treaty, the Bretton Woods accords, and the World Trade Organization (WTO) (pp. 728-729).

The research related well to the existing body of knowledge and extended the present body of knowledge with a contribution that was an original, current, extended survey and synthesis of the history and impact of international trade. There was no study research question, since this was not a study. The article's theoretical framework was appropriate and competent, as far as surveys go. The researchers clearly and fully communicated their results, which was essentially to prove that there were direct links between contemporary international issues and their origins traced, to the distinct periods discussed, to the early twentieth-century. There was no study method of research. There was no way to improve the research questions; this was a survey of the twentieth century, concerning international trade legislation and treaties, with how those period pieces related to current affairs in international trade. There were no controls. There was no research to replicate. The study's limitations were that the researchers did not conduct a study. Since this was a long literature survey, the rest of the study questions were rendered moot.

Crump, L. (2006). Competitively-linked and non-competitively-linked negotiations: Bilateral *trade policy* negotiations in Australia, Singapore and the United States. *International Negotiation, 11*(3), 431-466. Retrieved January 8, 2009, from Academic Search Premier database. (Accession Number: 23457141).

Crump (2006) drew a number of parallels between the art of negotiation, with respect to international trade, and the science of linking those negotiations to trade issues in general, and the necessary commodities and goods for trade, interregional or otherwise, in particular. As in the United States' domestic marketing channel, or the channels of most developed nations, there was a certain trade structure noted in this article that could be managed by multiple parties to include such previously mentioned international trade negotiations. Crump examined these issues, with relation to a variety of accords, and how those accords were manipulated by the parties to those accords. Examples of the accords discussed, for an explanation and delineation of the linkage relationships, were: the Singapore Free Trade Agreement of 2003 (USSFTA) and the Singapore-Australia Free Trade Agreement of 2003 (SAFTA) (p. 431).

The research related well to the existing body of knowledge and extended the present body of knowledge with a contribution that was an original, current, extended survey of international trade theory and marketing channel linkages. There was no study research question, since this was not a study. The article's theoretical framework was appropriate and competent, as far as surveys go. The researcher clearly and fully communicated his results, which was essentially to prove that there were relationships, or linkages, between trade policy and agreements to the channel movement of goods and commodities. There was no study method of research. There was no way to improve the research questions; this was a decision tree analysis for trade theory and relationships to marketing. There were no controls. There was no research to replicate. The study's limitations were that the researcher did not conduct a study. Since this was essentially a very long literature survey, the rest of the questions were rendered moot.

Dur, A. (2007). Foreign discrimination, protection for exporters, and U.S. *trade* liberalization. *International Studies Quarterly, 51*(2), 457-480. Retrieved January 8, 2009, from Academic Search Premier database. (Accession Number: 25558864).

Dur (2007) concluded that social and political implications were at the root of the diminishing levels of barriers to international trade in the United States. However, this was not determined to be the main reason behind the liberal tendencies associated with U.S. foreign trade. Special interest lobby groups were the proximal cause for the legislative moves toward the reduction of trade losses. The conclusion drawn by Dur, was that companies, that engaged in international trade, would mount lobbying pressure on the government's legislators to protect channel interests for the foreign trade distribution aspects. The European protectionism, of the three decades of the 1930s to the 1960s, tasked American companies to seek and obtain passage of critical legislation to protect trading interests in Europe. Those main bills passed, were the Trade Expansion Act (1962) and the Reciprocal Trade Agreements Act (1934) (p. 457).

The research related well to the existing body of knowledge and expanded that body of knowledge with a contribution that was original. The study's research questions were framed well and were significant. The study's theoretical framework was appropriate and related statistics of raw trade data to bills passed. The researcher clearly and fully communicated his results. The study's method of research was appropriate. There might be better research questions that could have been asked, but this would have meant changes to decades of raw data and the usage of passed bills as parameters. Controls used in the study were adequate, regarding bias of the researcher, and there was a sufficient size of the research sample employed in this study.

Confidence was high, if the samples of data and the same constraints were utilized, that the research should be replicable. The study's limitations were that the data were interpolated into bill passage rates, instead of trade rates increases or GDP output figures. The study's results should be reproducible and generalizable to economic trade policies for developed nations.

Faber, B. (2007). Towards the spatial patterns of sectoral adjustments to *trade* liberalisation: The case of NAFTA in Mexico. *Growth and Change, 38*(4), 567-594. Retrieved January 8, 2009, from Academic Search Premier database. (Accession Number: 27648211).

Faber (2007) discussed a variety of divergent theories and relationships, concerning the traditional trade theory implications of general trade theory's geospatial relationships, and their relationships to domestic trade; coupled with imports. The case in particular, explored by Faber, was the spatial trading regions within Mexico, compared with the imports from the United States. The crux of this study centered upon the relationships and differences, inter- and intra-regionally, compared with the adjusted tariffs structure and the mechanism for international trade associated with manufacturing distribution from the United States. The traditional Ricardian trade implications were compared and contrasted with traditional trade theory, through the use of decades of raw trade data and tariff percentage adjustments, to account for the domestic and international comparative advantage issues between nations in southern, North America (p. 567).

The research related well to the existing body of knowledge and expanded that body of knowledge with a contribution that was original. The study's research question was framed well and was significant. The study's theoretical framework was appropriate and related the raw trade data to tariff trade barriers figures and sanctions. The researcher clearly and fully communicated his results. The study's method of research was appropriate. There might be better research questions that could have been asked, but this would have meant a change in the use of decades of raw data, and the mathematics for tariff comparisons, regarding traditional trade relationships. Controls used in the study were adequate, regarding bias of the researcher, and there was a sufficient size of the research sample employed in this study.

If the samples of data and the same constraints were utilized, the research should be replicable. The study's limitations were that the data were confined to southern North American nations. The study's results should be reproducible and generalizable to North American trade.

Hurrell, A., & Narlikar, A. (2006). A new politics of confrontation? Brazil and India in multilateral *trade* negotiations. *Global Society: Journal of Interdisciplinary International Relations, 20*(4), 415-433. Retrieved January 8, 2009, from Academic Search Premier database. (Accession Number: 22908970).

Hurrell and Narlikar (2006) concluded that the world's developing nations, secondary to trade negotiations and the aspects of implied and enforced globalization, were resisting the trade policies of the developed nations. The Fourth and Third Worlds have come to the conclusion that trade policy could actually be utilized as foreign policy, and the use of treaties, agreements, and various enforced sanctions were used by the developing nations to secure better agreements and international trading advantages. India and Brazil were used as examples in this survey, and a literature synthesis, to demonstrate the use of trade policy as foreign policy to secure trading advantages and specific concessions to improve the longer term domestic issues, was associated with the economies of India and Brazil. The backdrop, provided for these policies, was the Cancun Conference and the nations' membership within the World Trade Organization (p. 415).

The research related well to the existing body of knowledge and extended the present body of knowledge with a contribution that was an original, current, extended survey of the world financial situation in international trade. There was no study research question, since this was not a study. The article's theoretical framework was appropriate and competent, as far as surveys go. The researchers clearly and fully communicated their results, which was essentially to demonstrate that international trade policy could be effectively used as national foreign policy. There was no study method of research. There was no way to improve the research questions; this was a survey of literature that discussed the developing countries' efforts to secure better trading relationships through policy enforcement. There were no controls. There was no research to replicate. The study's limitations were that the researchers did not conduct a study. Since this was essentially a very long literature survey, the rest of the questions were rendered moot.

Kneller, R. (2007). No miracles here: *Trade policy,* fiscal *policy* and economic growth. *Journal of Development Studies, 43*(7), 1248-1269. Retrieved January 8, 2009, from Academic Search Premier database. (Accession Number: 26952164).

Kneller (2007) noted in his study that there were relationships between the level of liberalized trade, and other economic indices, in the developing versus the developed countries. The critical factors considered were certain types of variables associated with the degree of trade, that was liberalized in the international arena, associated with the countries examined, and the other economic factors from the countries' aggregate economies: GDP growth; fiscal policy manifested as economic indices in general; and the effects of different types of growth that could actually be attributed to the aforementioned liberalization of international trade. Kneller noted that government interaction, within the international trade arena, could be econometrically predicted, or forecasted, and the quality, as well as the quantity, of trade policy liberalization had a direct impact upon a domestic economy's indices; over the long term. The conclusion was that, once fiscal policy was eliminated, no aggregate economic growth was experienced (p. 1248).

The research related well to the existing body of knowledge and expanded that body of knowledge with a contribution that was original. The study's research question was framed well and was significant. The study's theoretical framework was appropriate and related the statistics to expected GDP growth and fiscal policy considerations. The researcher clearly and fully communicated his results. The study's method of research was appropriate. There might be better research questions that could have been asked, but this would have meant a change to the data matrices and econometrics used in the study. Study controls were adequate, regarding bias of the researcher, and there was a sufficient size of the research sample employed in this study.

If the data samples and the constraints were re-utilized, the research should be replicable. The study's limitations were that the data were interpolated into fiscal policy regression data; by nation. The study's results should be reproducible and generalizable to developed nations.

Lavin, F. (2008). The social dimension of **trade**: The village blacksmith paradox. *Brown Journal of World Affairs, 14*(2), 241-251. Retrieved January 8, 2009, from Academic Search Premier database. (Accession Number: 32819055).

Lavin (2008) described a variety of critical changes to U.S. policies, concerning international trade, secondary to the Doha trade negotiations, and the curtailment of advocated and congressionally endorsed foreign trade policy. Although agreements for free trade were previously negotiated by U.S. Presidents, new administrations will be seriously weakened, with regard to the effectual negotiation of international trade treaties, because the U.S. Congress had just recently suspended the authority, for future administrations, to induce and promote such international trade. It seemed somewhat antiquated, with regard to trade ideology for the promotion of free trade and open international markets, for the resurgence of protectionism and protectionist ideals in the congress, when partisanship again made itself known with regard to legislation. Polls indicated that two-thirds of the American public favored protectionist policies in an era when it was noted that trade was critical to the aggregate U.S. economy (p. 241).

The research related well to the existing body of knowledge and expanded that body of knowledge with a contribution that was original. The study's research question was framed well and was significant. The study's theoretical framework was appropriate and related the statistics of trade to foreign policy. The researcher clearly and fully communicated his results. The study's method of research was appropriate. There might be better research questions that could have been asked, but this would have meant a change to the use of trade data and to the foreign trade policies, economically examined. Controls used in the study were adequate, regarding bias of the researcher, and there was a sufficient size of the research sample employed in this study.

If the samples of trade data and the same study constraints were utilized, the research should be replicable. The study's limitations were that the data were regressed against policy formulations. The study's results should be reproducible and generalizable to U.S. trade.

Leng, T. (2005). Commercial conflict and regulation in the discourse of trade in seventeenth-century England. *The Historical Journal, 48*(4), 933-954. Retrieved January 8, 2009, from Research Library database. (Document ID: 986982451).

Leng (2005) engaged in a prolonged discourse of trade and national foreign policy, which had occurred in the 1600s of England's colonial period. The author sought to provide an intellectual platform for international trade policy and regulation, for the seventeenth-century, in order to draw parallels to contemporary England, and the world's developing nations. Leng's survey provided a number of cases in point, which could have been aptly applied to current affairs and contemporary policy formulations, regarding trade policy and the use of foreign trade as national foreign policy. Protectionism and a variety of trade sanctions were discussed, in order to provide the foundation, which was the nature of the survey's intent. Although there were any number of startling policy parallels, which were revealed from antiquity, as they related to contemporarily developed, national, fiscal policy, most of the discourse could have been taken directly from a graduate level, economic history text (p. 933).

The research related well to the existing body of knowledge and extended the present body of knowledge with a contribution that was an original, current, extended survey of the parallels between seventeenth-century, colonial England and the present. There was no study research question, since this was not a study. The article's theoretical framework was appropriate and competent, as far as surveys go. The researcher clearly and fully communicated his results, which was essentially to demonstrate parallels between colonial England's foreign trade policies and those associated with the present. There was no study method of research. There was no way to improve the research questions; this was an economic survey of colonial, versus contemporary England's, trade policies and foreign policy. There were no controls. There was no research to replicate. The study's limitations were that the researcher did not conduct a study. Since this was essentially a very long literature survey, the rest of the questions were rendered moot.

Lobell, S. (2004). Historical lessons to extend America's great power tenure. *World Affairs, 166*(4), 175-184. Retrieved January 8, 2009, from Research Library database. (Document ID: 597812861).

Lobell (2004) discussed a number of antiquated strategy lessons, in his economic history literature survey, which he concluded could serve as models for contemporary, American, foreign policy, with regard to governmental fiscal policy associated with international trade. The three models that Lobell discussed in this survey were: royal decrees associated with the Spanish dominion of trade in the era of 1621-1640; the cooperative nature of foreign policy, concerning international trade, followed by the P.M. during England's concessionist epoch of 1932-1939; and the specific political fiscal policy formulations, mixed with military responses, keyed to the British epoch of 1889-1912. A variety of parallels were drawn by Lobell for the formulation of American trade policy, secondary to foreign policy considerations, to reward, punish, or improve relations with potential trading partners in the international trade arena (p. 175).

The research related well to the existing body of knowledge and extended the present body of knowledge with a contribution that was an original, current, extended survey of the foreign policy and international trade implications of models for such trade, provided by economic history. There was no study research question, since this was not a study. The article's theoretical framework was appropriate and competent, as far as surveys go. The researcher clearly and fully communicated his results, which was essentially to provide historical examples from economic history for future foreign policy and trade formulations for American policy. There was no study method of research. There was no way to improve the research questions; this was basically an economic history lesson for contemporary, American diplomats and trade officials. There were no controls. There was no research to replicate. The study's limitations were that the researcher did not conduct a study. Since this was essentially a very long, economic history, literature survey, the rest of the questions were rendered moot.

Lobell, S. (2008). The second face of American security: The US-Jordan free trade agreement as security policy. *Comparative Strategy, 27*(1), 88-100. Retrieved January 8, 2009, from Academic Search Premier database. (Accession Number: 31168067).

Lobell (2008) noted that developed countries pursued foreign policies, through the use of political and economic strategies that manifested into such policies, to make smaller nations subservient and obedient to the economic will of those larger nations. One of the means of access to the smaller countries, through the manipulation of their international trade access and markets, was determined to be through the use of policies of international trade that manifested through agreements and treaties. The passive means of using this type of political and economic force on smaller nations was noted to be security's secondary face, whereas the primary means of bullying, through the use of military saber-rattling or restrictive trade policies, was security's primary face. The basic model that was given by example was the instance of the Washington, D.C. model, as applied to the nation-state of Jordan in the Middle East. The purpose of this policy was ostensibly to stabilize the region in general, and to support the diplomatic relationship with Israel in particular (p. 88).

The research related well to the existing body of knowledge and extended the present body of knowledge with a contribution that was an original, current, extended survey of the world financial situation. There was no study research question, since this was not a study. The article's theoretical framework was appropriate and competent, as far as surveys go. The researcher clearly and fully communicated his results, which was essentially to prove the difference, by example, between the secondary and primary faces of national security. There was no study method of research. There was no way to improve the research questions; this was basically a re-hash of current events to prove the two points. There were no controls. There was no research to replicate. The study's limitations were that the researcher did not conduct a study. Since this was essentially a very long literature survey, the rest of the questions were moot.

Looney, R. (2004). Petroeuros: A threat to U.S. interests in the gulf? *Middle East Policy, 11*(1), 26-37. Retrieved January 8, 2009, from Research Library database. (Document ID: 611327931).

Looney (2004) mentioned that approximately three-quarters of the international repositories of liquid capital (about 70%), for this example, currency for international trading that a country would utilize for security from arbitrage, was held in the form of American dollars. Due to the security provided by such stable currency supplies, particularly in the form of U.S. dollars, nations were able to maintain equilibrium and conduct foreign trade internationally without adverse effects to their domestic economies. The author contended that Hussein was deposed from rule in Iraq due to the fact that he de-stabilized the entire region through conversion of currency acceptance: Hussein demanded and received euros, instead of U.S. dollars for Iraqi oil sales starting in the year 2000. Looney's contention was that the continued use of the euro for petroleum purchases would continue to de-stabilize the region, and eventually the world, because there was not enough of a supply of euros and there was not enough of a supply of the euro as currency, in order to effectively conduct such commerce effectively (p. 26).

The research related well to the existing body of knowledge and extended the present body of knowledge with a contribution that was an original, current, extended survey of the international trade associated with petroleum and currency issues secondary to that. There was no study research question, since this was not a study. The article's theoretical framework was appropriate and competent, as far as surveys go. The researcher clearly and fully communicated his results, which was essentially to demonstrate dollar security and instability in oil exports. There was no study method of research. There was no way to improve the research questions; this was basically an international trade, strategy paper. There were no controls.

There was no research to replicate. The study's limitations were that the researcher did not conduct a study. Since this was essentially a very long literature survey, the rest of the questions were moot.

Meunier, S., & Nicolaidis, K. (2006). The European Union as a conflicted trade power. *Journal of European Public Policy, 13*(6), 906-925. Retrieved January 8, 2009, from Academic Search Premier database. (Accession Number: 21806746).

Meunier and Nicolaidis (2006) contended that the European Union was the strongest trade interest in international trade, because of the number of nations involved, thus having demonstrated raw buying power, and because of the four decades of experience with trade agreements from all over Europe. The authors also contended that the trading bloc was starting to develop power in the political arena as well. Further, the bloc has started to expect, demand, and receive changes to domestic policies, as a result of its trade. These changes were accorded to small issues, such as labor, but were sometimes larger concessions such as the conduct of policies, foreign and domestic, and political concessions in international policies as well. The article discussed the three main areas of economic power afforded to the EU: structural, bargaining, and trade. The conclusion of the article noted that the EU would have to adjust the exercise, or use of such economic power, in order to move from the basics of structural economic power to something that was an acceptable means of international trade conduct (p. 906).

The research related well to the existing body of knowledge and extended the present body of knowledge with a contribution that was an original, current, extended survey of the international trade power of the EU. There was no study research question, since this was not a study. The article's theoretical framework was appropriate and competent, as far as surveys go. The researchers clearly and fully communicated their results, which was essentially to prove the existence of the three types of trade power wielded by the EU. There was no study method of research. There was no way to improve the research questions; this was basically a literature survey of the economics of interregional, EU trade. There were no controls. There was no research to replicate. The study's limitations were that the researchers did not conduct a study. Since this was essentially a very long economics literature survey, the rest of the questions were rendered moot.

Naim, M. (2003). The five wars of globalization. *Foreign Policy, 134*(1), 28-36. Retrieved January 8, 2009, from ABI/INFORM Global database. (Document ID: 278453641).

Naim (2003) advocated a discussion concerning globalization and five worldwide conflicts, which were currently being fought, concerning the spread of globalization. The article was a strategic survey of the five wars, associated with the spread of globalization: the spread of illegal weapons; the smuggling of human, chattel labor; the spread and sales of illegal drugs; the spread and sales of illegal, phony products, such as music CDs; and the spread of counterfeit currency. The article contended that these five international issues were not much separately, with regard to their impact upon international trade, but their collective impact upon world trade, over the past ten years, has absolutely skyrocketed. There were many potential problems and issues cited in the article, concerning these issues and their cumulative effects upon the world markets. The largest issue with these five wars, and the global trade arena, was the combined costs to international trade and the asset depletion to pay those associated costs (pp. 29-30).

The research related well to the existing body of knowledge and extended the present body of knowledge with a contribution that was an original, current, extended survey of the world situation concerning the permeation of illegal trade. There was no study research question, since this was not a study. The article's theoretical framework was appropriate and competent, as far as surveys go. The researcher clearly and fully communicated his results, which was essentially to prove that there were five fronts, in the global trade arena, that presented a war upon illegal trade, which was fought by most nations. There was no study method of research. There was no way to improve the research questions; this was basically a summary of the five illegal wars' fronts, and how nations were paying for the trade resolutions. There were no controls. There was no research to replicate. The study's limitations were that the researcher did not conduct a study. Since this was essentially a literature survey; the study questions were moot.

Reichert, M., & Jungblut, B. (2007). European Union external *trade policy*: Multilevel principal–agent relationships. *Policy Studies Journal, 35*(3), 395-418. Retrieved January 8, 2009, from Academic Search Premier database. (Accession Number: 27230504).

Reichert and Jungblut (2007) determined that the European Union had gained a tremendous amount of influence, with respect to the volume and value of international trade, and that an improved understanding of the EU's method for external trade would promote a better understanding of international trade in general. The article surveyed a number of current literature pieces and promoted the idea that the EU evaluated, from a domestic, as well as an international policy perspective, four critical parts of the trade structure, in order to formulate trade policies: "selection;" "incentive;" "monitoring;" and "sanctions." The approximately two dozen countries affiliated as members of the EU, as a trading bloc, each had their own particular mix of these generalized parts of the evaluation structure for trade, but the authors contended that these were the four specific guidelines utilized by the domestic governments of the EU to formulate fiscal and trade policies for the conduct of domestic and international trade (p. 395).

The research related well to the existing body of knowledge and extended the present body of knowledge with a contribution that was an original, current, extended survey of the world financial situation, with regard to trade promulgated by the twenty-five EU nations. There was no study research question, since this was not a study. The article's theoretical framework was appropriate and competent, as far as surveys go. The researchers clearly and fully communicated their results, which was essentially to prove that there four points to the evaluation and formulation for the trade conducted by the nations who were members of the EU. There was no study method of research. There was no way to improve the research questions; this was basically a summary of the EU trade structure. There were no controls. There was no research to replicate. The study's limitations were that the researchers did not conduct a study. Since this was essentially a literature survey, the rest of the questions were rendered moot.

Young, A., & Peterson, J. (2006). The EU and the new *trade* politics. *Journal of European Public Policy, 13*(6), 795-814. Retrieved January 8, 2009, from Academic Search Premier database. (Accession Number: 21806745).

Young and Peterson (2006) noted that the political outlook, of the two dozen, European Union nations, has changed the manner in which those countries used the politics associated with trade in the international arena. The first factor, which has changed recently, has to do with domestic issues associated with the movements of capital and the institution of trade policy. The second change has been with regard to the actual interplay of microeconomic institutions, NGOs, and the formulation of government policy. The third change has been to the manner in which EU nations have been regarded and treated by the developing nations of the world, with regard to such policies, their formulation, and the conduct of international trade. Domestic governments in the EU have started to respond to these international, changing conditions, by altering the intrinsic reasons for their international trade, and their ideas about what those changes will mean in the immediate future, domestically, within the respective, member EU nations (p. 795).

The research related well to the existing body of knowledge and extended the present body of knowledge with a contribution that was an original, current, extended survey of the European Union nations and their international trade policies. There was no study research question, since this was not a study. The article's theoretical framework was appropriate and competent, as far as surveys go. The researchers clearly and fully communicated their results, which was essentially to prove that there were three major changes occurring in the formulation of domestic governance and trade policy formulation in the EU nations. There was no study method of research. There was no way to improve the research questions; this was basically a strategy survey. There were no controls. There was no research to replicate. The study's limitations were that the researchers did not conduct a study. Since this was essentially a literature survey of strategic trade options, the rest of the questions were rendered moot.

Literature Review Essay

Introduction

This literature review essay builds upon the theoretical perspectives and critical analyses presented in the Breadth component of this paper by using those international trade theorists, and the applicable parts of their respective theories, as a foundation for the discussion involving the current research that was introduced in the annotations above. The integrated focus of the annotated research articles discussed above was international trade theory as it relates to the development of international trade, national foreign policy, and the conduct of trade internationally among nations and to the development of a platform of values that is useful in international trade as it relates to international trade theory, national foreign policy, and the conduct of trade internationally among nations. The outline of the organization of this literature survey includes major aspects of international trade theory and contemporary developments of specific concepts in international trade theory and how those concepts relate to practical applications of international trade theory, national foreign policy, and the conduct of trade internationally among nations: international trade and the mechanics of statecraft; international trade structural linkages in treaty negotiations; international trade regulation as a response to export discrimination;

intranational and international adjustments to liberalized, international trade; trade politics and foreign policy in multi-lateral international trade; trade liberalization and economic growth in developing countries; protectionism, restrictions, and barriers to contemporary international trade; mercantilist commercial policy and the regulation of international trade; classic, economic history, policy responses to international trade challenges; uses of economic statecraft to foster secondary state, international trade support; the use of U.S. dollars as the international currency for oil, international trade; the exercise of the European Union's trade power in international trade; the five wars of international trade resulting from the spread of globalization; influences on the European Union's external trade policy; and the Deep Trade Agenda, trade politics, and market integration of the European Union.

The rationale of the Depth narrative is to explore in detail these fifteen named aspects of international trade theory, and contemporary developments of specific concepts in international trade theory, and how those concepts relate to practical applications of international trade theory, national foreign policy, and the conduct of trade internationally among nations. Analysis of the various contemporary developments of the specific concepts in international trade theory and how those concepts relate to practical applications of international trade theory, national foreign policy, and the conduct of trade internationally, is provided with relation to the theories espoused in the Breadth segment, to improve the reader's understanding of these subjects and to provide a foundation for analysis, comparison, and contrast in the Application segment of this paper.

International Trade and the Mechanics of Statecraft

The part one synthesis discussed the progression of the state, with regard to statecraft's evolution, in the years after World War One. The parallels were drawn between the statesmanship practiced by the United States, Japan, and the different evolved democracies in the European theater. The discussion had some remarkable ideas concerning goals that were considered, at the time, to be synthetic or perhaps even far-fetched. However, the basic soundness, from political stand-points, was borne out over time and the remedial changes to political policies, foreign and domestic, continued to astound economic historians.

The part two synthesis had more to do with the practical aspects of the statesmanship previously discussed above. Although it was noted that there were profound changes occurring throughout the world, and that strategy and the structural nature of international law were malleable, due to the arrangements made between and among countries, these were the solitary issues for contention. The contention issues depended upon the total structure for enforcement and the nature of the state changed considerably after World War Two to include more of the developed and developing world. The larger parts of the world were enveloped by the expanding international trade arena, but not all of the nations advanced at the same rate.

The part three synthesis was an ideological reversion to the old comparative advantage lectures secondary to Ricardian trade theory. The discussion focused upon the sort of discussion that was antiquated and it ante-dated general trade theory. However, the discussion quickly advanced into the twenty-first century with a discussion concerning how new paradigms were necessary in the international trade arena and a sort of enhanced structure, with a new type of trade language, was needed to advance trade interests for countries around the world. The discussion centered upon the new needs for trade, with the collapse of the 1940s Bretton Woods system in the 1970s, and how that new structure was beginning to evolve in the new millennium. The closing remarks focused upon the new opportunities of an uncertain international trade future for all nations (Afilalo and Patterson, 2006).

International Trade Structural Linkages in Treaty Negotiations

The contemporary literature survey found that it was not unusual for international trade negotiations to be linked to other such trade negotiations. In fact, the structural mechanism of the negotiating environment, for such negotiations of international trade agreements and treaties, actually was shown to promote such linkages. Part of the reason and rationale for such treaty and agreement linkages was due to the effective policy promulgation of the effectiveness, usefulness, and trade strategy associated with such linkages. Another reason for such linkages was due to the fact that trade negotiations were conducted by numerous parties and each party wanted some participation in the evolution of the treaties or agreements that followed. Further, the groups of negotiators, that evolve, secondary to such negotiations, made it a point to link the negotiations for mutual benefit. Thus, the combination of trade strategy and linkages, in international trade, created an atmosphere of competition, due to the association of each separate party and the extent of the participation or lack of it in the negotiations.

The literature begged the question: if the international trade arena were an environment that was a situation where negotiators competed for advantage, would the previously mentioned linkages be evident? Then it proceeded to speak of linkages that were not so obvious, and what it would presumably take to label them in treaties or agreements. There were further questions concerning whether the linkages, that were evident or embedded in the treaty language, could possibly affect the strength of the negotiators involved. It was noted that the linkages that were not obvious, could adversely affect other negotiations, and the results could be modified to a position not in favor of the associated negotiator. It was further noted that linkages could be re-arranged or even disappear as career negotiators moved to other positions or eventually retired from the service.

The topics that preoccupied negotiators, in the previous international trade negotiation rounds of talks, were: issues concerning banking, in order to control certain types of capital movement in foreign countries; issues concerning the sales, internationally, of fiduciary and financial instruments; the institution of sanctions, such as tariffs, and what those percentages might be; international banking licenses, so that banks could be sold internationally to foreign interests or other countries; international trade non-compete agreements, so that nations could promote trade and receive more of a certain type of that trade; and agreements regarding telecommunications.

It was demonstrated that many factors contributed to the dynamics associated with the linkages involved with international treaty and agreement negotiations. Sometimes, it was noted, that the smallest factor could change the direction of the negotiations, down an irreversible path. However, the contention was brought to the fore, that the development of trade coalitions was the most effective means of changing the nature of the negotiations in progress, to exercise trade power and alter the potential outcome of those negotiations (Crump, 2006).

International Trade Regulation as a Response to Export Discrimination

The current literature noted that society, along with the rigors of the political environment, expected American authorities to minimize the number and associated amounts of international trade sanctions since the end of the Great Depression. However, the studies were unable to determine the exact nature of the structure or of the impact moments of such reductions, due to the liberal nature of trade occurring since the 1930s. The research concluded that special interest groups have pursued legislation that supported the minimization of shortfalls in trade, instead of legislation that supported ease of penetration into the international markets.

The special interest groups that supported international trade were usually ready to make an inroad to the Beltway establishment, in Washington, D.C., in order to make certain that there would be a minimum of foiled trading agreements with foreign powers so that trade goods continued to be exported around the world. The literature noted examples of trade legislation, which was passed to reduce or eliminate foreign trade barriers in other nations, that was passed in the era from the end of the Great Depression well into the first Nixon Administration.

The literature demonstrated that there was, already in existence, over seven decades of legislation that had proceeded to reduce the levels of impediments, concerning the various types of tariff based walls to international trade, when compared with the era depicted by the 1930s. It was noted that, sometimes, the nature of a trade agreement's arbitrary nature made the eventual economic results difficult to imagine. Although inroads have been made, with respect to the reduction of trade barriers, it was revealed that domestic governments occasionally instituted legislation that could impede the progress made by the international accords. It was shown that it was impossible to determine, even with preferential trading agreements, which companies would be able to capitalize on those agreements, due to consumer preferences in the nation that imported the goods. Part of the notion of barriers in general stemmed from Britain, during the Great Depression, the largest importer of goods from America, which lifted walls to virtually all non-British goods for importation. The by-product of this trade wall, from England, was reflected in the trade policies of Canada, toward U.S. imports, which dramatically reduced the importation of goods from the U.S. into Canada during the Great Depression.

At the beginning of the Kennedy Administration, the European nations created the EFTA, or European Free Trade Association, which allowed the seven member nations to discriminate against U.S. imports. Therefore, the activity in the trade walls raised, in the 1930s and the 1960s, contributed to the special interest groups' increased levels of activity lobbying in those time periods. Part of the solution to trade barriers, was determined to be reciprocal treaties and other forms of agreements, which would help to reduce trade walls and sanctions against the U.S. The U.S. and England held trade conferences, near the end of World War Two, in order to dissolve the barriers previously erected to U.S. exports. These sorts of trade meetings were demonstrated to have resolved issues with many nations, such as through the implementation of the Trade Expansion Act, in order drop trade walls and barriers to international trade with the United States (Dur, 2007).

Intranational and International Adjustments to Liberalized, International Trade

The literature noted that there were a variety of new models, which had been introduced as models concerned with the geospatial economics of a nation's aggregate economy. These models were designed to address the intranational distinctions of an economy, as opposed to the international aspects of international trade for that economy, with respect to liberalized trade. The main question addressed in the new models, concerning the intranational trade, was with respect to the nature of the traditional two part model that only included manufacturing and agriculture. The real aspect examined was whether or not the total manufacturing output increased due to trade liberalization. Similar to general trade theory, the new models considered grouping differences that were related to the geospatial nature of trade liberalization.

The literature discussed a ten-year study that depicted a manufacturing center in Mexico that demonstrated better international trade availability that promoted improved intranational trade and international trade. This was opposed to areas that had ineffective access to international trade; those poor access areas had reduced intranational trade and production, in spite of a natural propensity for comparative advantage secondary to the manufacturing of trade goods. The spatial aspect of international trade was demonstrated by the fact that more than 80 percent of the total trade with Mexico, exported to Mexico and imported by the United States, was conducted over the terrain lines shared with the U.S. This was an assumption that was rigorously examined, with regard to the volume and value of NAFTA, during the empirical data examination of the groupings assembled for the period of the ten-year study (1993-2003). Part of that study was the geospatial aspects of the treaty's effects, secondary to the coalescing of international trade across borders in North America.

When the new trade models were examined, the linkages of the trade, not considering transportation costs, showed the increased movement of goods in both directions over the borders. There were minor fluxes in the numbers, due to the permutations associated with the use of open versus closed trade models, but the percentage differences were negligible. Some of the factors assessed, were the impact on the manufacturing trade compared with an immobile population of labor and the different linkages associated with the improved trade versus the static nature of poor trade access in the different geospatial areas under examination. Some of the areas did have better trade volume, secondary to better comparative advantage issues. An over-arching consideration, when the trade was examined with respect to the gravity model of trade, was the distance between hubs, regarding transportation costs and the associated value of such trade. Over two-dozen geographic areas were examined, and the trade distance was shown to be a factor. Thus, it was no surprise when it was demonstrated that the half-dozen, northern Mexican areas, proximal to the U.S. border, grew at higher rates, with regard to international trade, than the further inland areas in the study. The real key to North American cross-border increases, in international trade, seemed to be the location, comparative advantage issues, and the free-trade access to the U.S. border (Faber, 2007).

Trade Politics and Foreign Policy in Multi-Lateral International Trade

It was noted, that the domestic governmental trade formulations, were only a part of the overall trade situation. The real issues, for international trade, stemmed from intermittent changes in the foreign political formulations, by the respective governments to the trades, concerning the actual trade issues seen as foreign policy. In the recent trade negotiations, for the Doha round, the overall agenda for the international trade issues was actually deferred by the developing countries, until their trade demands were met by the developed nations. These policy blockages were seen to have arisen from the American and European trade accords (Blair House), which was observed to have diminished the trade available to the developing nations. Although there were a number of countries that had felt slighted, and their issues were extremely dissimilar, the developing nations banded together in order to block the passage of the accords in the international trade, Doha round.

The movement toward the group based issues, from the research based agendas, was seen to replace the more traditional negotiating formats. Thus, the developing nations' coalitions were able to use the research from their studies to stall the passage of crucial agreements; this stone-walled the developed nations' negotiating teams. The other issue, associated with the trade agreement blockages, was that the developing nations' coalition framed their formulations in the language of the WTO, instead of in the more traditional language of former agreement propositions. The developing nations comprise a substantial group of countries that have banded together to assert their influence on trade negotiations. Attempts to separate these powers, with a variety of tactics, have proven to be unsuccessful and they maintain a considerable solidarity. Some scholars have attempted to explain away these tactics with references to domestic policy, but the coalition endures, and is a force to be reckoned with at the trade negotiations tables. NGOs were shown to be amenable to the coalition studies presented. The strength of the developing country coalition continues to grow, and they will continue to be a force at the international trade, trading tables at further WTO trade rounds (Hurrell and Narlikar, 2006).

Trade Liberalization and Economic Growth in Developing Countries

Studies have demonstrated that the growth rate of the economy, and GDP output, increased after the advent of trade liberalization in developing countries. This growth was shown to be tied to the formulation and use of fiscal policy on behalf of the domestic governments examined. To properly calibrate and examine the empirical data, concerned with trade liberalization in the affected developing countries, the times of the time periods under investigation were in groups of five years each: the period before trade liberalization; the period during the associated liberalization; and the period after such liberalization was reported to have occurred. Although there were six distinct areas that could have been examined, with regard to liberalization and growth, the divergent path under investigation, was the aspect of fiscal policy formulation advanced by the developing countries' governments.

Although the trending was indicated to be upward, for both types of countries under examination, the trade liberalized and the non-liberalized, the cumulative economic growth rate for both types of countries was almost synonymous; the rates were extremely close, statistically. Even when these data were regressed, there was an indication of stronger growth, associated with the developing nations that liberalized their international trade in the late 1980s. Further, the significant growth occurred, in those designated countries, for a period of only about five to ten years after that period of trade liberalization of the late 1980s.

The literature suggested, after the turn of the millennium, that the degree of trade freedom and openness did have something to do with GDP growth and the formulation of the associated domestic fiscal policy, in the developing countries examined. It was found that greater trade openness and freedom promoted growth, but the growth declined because fiscal policy formulation promoted social services spending that reduced the net result from the increased growth. It was found that lower degrees of openness and trade freedom reduced the economic growth and actually decreased government spending, as demonstrated by fiscal policy formulation, and still resulted in lower growth rates; just like trade openness and trade freedom. Therefore, the consideration of a more controlled, government fiscal policy that could conceivably promote growth associated with trade liberalization seemed to be understood, but not realized. It was demonstrated, however, that non-liberalizing countries experienced lower spending on non-social services programs, than the trade liberalized countries.

The results noted that the formulation of fiscal policy actually concealed the benefits experienced by the economy, resulting from trade liberalization, in developing countries. When fiscal policy was discounted from the equations, there was no significant difference between trade liberalized and the non-trade liberalized countries, with respect to aggregate economic performance, of their domestic economies. Thus, the conclusion was that fiscal policy formulation, by the domestic government of a developing country, had a significant effect upon the net growth rate of the aggregate, national economy (Kneller, 2007).

Protectionism, Restrictions, and Barriers to Contemporary International Trade

The United States enjoyed, in fiscal 2007, the highest percentage of GDP growth, also the most significant in the form of U.S. dollars, as a result of trade exports. Part of the reason for this was attributed to the fact that foreign corporations obtained access to the U.S. trading market, and as a direct result, all of the markets with whom the U.S., as a nation, trades. So, the free trade policies tended to feed upon themselves and grow, promoting participation and interest from foreign companies. With regard to trade shortfalls, concerning imports, those imports promote lower costs for inputs to manufacturing, more buying opportunities for American consumers, and a reduction in economic indices; namely inflation. Unfortunately, high percentages of the U.S. shortfalls in trade are attributable to nations with which America does not have a free trade agreement (84 %). Laughingly, it was demonstrated that those who criticized trade shortfalls did not approve of or support free trade treaties; a seeming contradiction of ideologies.

There seems to be a great deal of confusion in international trade, supported by a plethora of examples; since American trade negotiators felt that the country of South Korea wasn't proactive about the marketing of U.S. beef products, the rest of the trade intended for South Korea was suspended. Partisanship also reared its head when the President sought to move a vote forward, concerning the country of Colombia and international trade, even though Democrats sought to delay or prevent it completely. There did not seem to much sense in the actions taken by congress, when it was alluded to that it would support token trade measures, but not those that brought in the most revenue from exports for the United States' home interests.

The overall structural aspects of the trade system seem to be affecting the ability of the individual nations to perform and conduct trade. The efficiency of the system, since adequate reserves and choices were not made, due to the new supply chain issues associated with smaller inventories and instant deliveries, have adversely affected the additional trade order associated with the repetitive and surplus supply issues of previous times. Although smaller industries and companies have a stronger social identity, the times have changed to where nameless and faceless entities perform the ordering and supply of commodities. Free trade agreements have provided anonymity to the ordering and supply sides of the economy, but the literature indicated that some time will pass before the integration issues are resolved with respect to the new trends in international trade (Lavin, 2008).

Mercantilist Commercial Policy and the Regulation of International Trade

The economic history literature surveyed, indicated that mercantilist England was characterized by businesspeople and politicians that saw trade as a winning or losing proposition. In other words, parties to a trade were delineated by the labels of *winner* or *loser*, and that the concept of *win-win* international trading seemed to have been a recent development. Thus, the antiquated ideology of the mercantilists was described by the rigors of competing for goods and was held as secondary to communicating the market's needs. The vying for goods, in the international markets, began to erode sentiment for England, and the political and jurisprudence establishments intervened, concerning international trade intercourse. The over-arching idea associated with mercantilism in general was that it characterized international commerce as aggressive and menacing and that the nature of commerce called out for structure from jurists or for fiscal policy.

The practical link associated with the mercantilist school of theory was linked to the belief system that espoused the use of specie. It seemed obvious to mercantilists that when specie was exchanged for goods, there was inevitably a winner and loser, as parties to any trade transaction. Thus, since trade was viewed as one large corpus, then all trades were shown to be profitable in a single direction, due to the fact that what one person acquired, another was bound to have lost. Incredibly, the government supported this line of thinking and passed fiscal policy to support this line of thought in the conduct of international trade. The literature advanced the notion that this was the main reason behind the ascendance of the Dutch traders on the world markets in the seventeenth century. If the Dutch were then to be utilized as a model for the expert management of trade practices, then England was gradually seen to become the warehouser, for the conduct of trade, since she inevitably sought to warehouse the more important commodities to put the nation into the heart of much of the trade then extant.

There was a movement to align Dutch and English interests, so that the practices of the Dutch would dovetail with the warehousing of the English, but the agreement failed to pass. The proposed agreement would have eliminated a great deal of economic friction between the two nations, with regard to the winning and losing application of international trade, so that neither the Dutch nor the English would have experienced a loss in trades. There were agreements that passed, through fiscal policy determinations, but they did not align the Dutch and English interests. The agreements did, however, provide a modicum of insulation from the Dutch, without reliance on commercial trading companies.

Some of the literature indicated that the Dutch trade ascendancy occurred due to the international reliance upon their navigation. The eventual development of Dutch shipping, supporting the carriage of goods internationally among nations, contributed to this trade ascendancy, which forced many countries to rely solely upon the Dutch for imports. Thus, the Dutch were in a position to slice prices and move against any competition, enforcing pseudo-monopolies in many areas. The British were able to compete based upon trade with her numerous colonies, so the Dutch were not able to close the British out of the international trade arena completely. International trade was being set into position to change yet again, when economic strength began to be identified with population centers and mass, so that the British began to rely more heavily upon colonies for agricultural might (Leng, 2005).

Classic, Economic History, Policy Responses to International Trade Challenges

The first scenario, described as the ideal promulgated of the disciplining of wayward powers, was the era of the Spaniards, who held world sway, from 1621-1640. In essence, the Spaniards fought all of the known powers at the time, the: Swedes; Turks; English; French; and even the Dutch. To add to the confusion and foment, these powers were embattled by the Spaniards, usually at the same time, and even on several different fronts of battle. The survey noted that there were a number of internal battles; the internal strife caused by the marginal successes in the worldwide scavenging for resources and cash, which lead to the diminished capabilities for the determination of government policy and the marginalized martial might.

The second scenario, which was characterized by the British appeasement stance of 1932-1939, or a sort of nervous cooperative nature, was on the part of England's foreign policy and trade agreements. Although the axis powers, at the time Italy, Japan, and Germany, were obtaining more and more territory through ignominious subterfuges, or other nefarious methods, the British had hoped to avoid a World War with their foreign and trade policies of appeasement. Unfortunately, although many pundits reasoned that war was actually inevitable, Britain was not quite in a war-ready stance, because war preparations were not pursued vigorously internally, secondary to the policies pursued externally. Unfortunately, due to several somewhat questionable agreements on military might trades and international trade, Britain was in the uncomfortable position of having to bypass the renegotiation or the extended new agreements, to which it had originally agreed.

The third scenario, was also dominated by the British, as a world power, from 1889-1912 and was characterized by a sort of de-evolution of big government; on a micro scale. England was amenable to measures brought by the United States, Japan, and France, which succeeded in decreasing the international status of Russia and Germany with the use of structural programs to increase sea might, increase the use of trade sanctions, and promote treaties that preferred other countries for international trade. This was the strategy that England used for several decades to guarantee her military might and the resources reserve to promote domestic and international government policy promulgation (Lobell, 2004).

Uses of Economic Statecraft to Foster Secondary State, International Trade Support

The literature observed that super-power, developed nations have utilized policy formulation strategies to arrange supportive, international trade responses from nations located in critical geographic areas of the world. There was some theoretical contention that trading treaties and agreements could be used to anticipate or foster supportive policy formulations, from the geographically strategic states, to promote cooperative policy in critical areas of the world; policies beneficial to the economics and trade of developed nation super-powers. A more direct example of this filling of the power-vacuum in an area of the Middle East, was the American fiscal and trade policies with the country of Jordan, in order to foster better relations with the country of Israel. A key component of these surveys was the fourth protocol, known as the promotion of international trade policy, and those associated trade treaties, as part and parcel an adjunct to national policy concerning home security.

Part of the issue, associated with trade policy's use as a tool of national security, was the retaliation of special interest groups in the region; certain factions in the Middle East that did not approve of these policy incursions. The evolution of trade agreements has been proven to foster the position of conservatives and of regional leaders in Jordan. This strength has emanated from agreements such as: the U.S.-Jordan Free Trade Agreement in 2001; and the subsidy and establishment of Qualified Industrial Zones in 1996 (Lobell, 2008).

These types of agreements were not endorsed by those with a global bent, since these factions were proponents of economic equilibrium, cheap security determinations, indiscriminant contact with other nations, and the antiquated policies already posited, with regard to policy formulations in the financial monetary and governmental fiscal establishments. The types of factions that supported such antiquated, establishmentarian mores were identified as: central planning enterprises; bureaucrats and tenured employees; manufacturing and agribusiness concerns that were already deemed inefficient; and hackneyed firms that promoted cheap imports. The scenario was reminiscent of the seventeenth century mercantilist pundits who touted a winner and loser in every trade transaction. Obviously, there were a great many groups of society that were going to be examined and affected, with some friction directly attributed to the trade policies that caused the groups' discomforts.

The Jordan situation was examined in the literature, because United Nations trade barriers hurt the economy of the region in general and Jordan in particular. Some of the issues, identified as troublesome to Jordan secondary to the sanctions, were: minimized geospatial trade throughout the region; market reduction and trade loss; and loss of aid and subsidized loans. Part of the United States' aid to Jordan, as a result of the treaties and agreements, included: the removal of central authority control from critical industries, such as manufacturing, transportation, and communication; the westernization of certain economic indices and reporting techniques; and wealth re-distribution to former, centrally-controlled areas.

It was noted that Palestine was fostering a business class, which emerged in Jordan as a result of the westernized regulation and policy induction. These Palestinian businesspeople were described to be a sort of new-regime, Middle Eastern *yuppie*, who was educated outside of the region, younger than the former elites, and was extremely eager to negotiate agreements with foreign interests; including the inclusion of Israeli companies as venture partners to international trade. Traditional Jordanian interests controlled the central planning bureaucracy, but the newly ascended Palestinians, and their trade establishments, dominated the non-public arena, which included international commerce and the finance secondary to the use of banks. Free Trade Agreements had a higher degree of acceptance when the agreement was free from the conditionality aspects of fiscal and foreign adjustments to policy formulation. This was shown to minimize western, ideological rejection and Islamic, social retribution (Lobell, 2008).

The Use of U.S. Dollars as the International Currency for Oil, International Trade

There were six basic reasons for the promotion of the U.S. dollar as petroleum currency world-wide. The first reason was directly in line with the American interest in fostering the U.S. dollar as a medium of exchange. Since the foreign powers that purchased petroleum, just like the United States, needed money to spend, it was in the interest of American interests abroad, to have those purchases made with U.S. dollars. In this way, when foreign nations were looking for venues for capital investment, the money would return home to American interests. The second reason, although it may have seemed obvious, was that when the American currency did eventually make its way back to America, since it was already in the home currency, the risks attributable to currency exchange were virtually zero. The third reason was that when the U.S. dollars returned to America, that capital would then be invested in American investment interests. It didn't particularly matter whether those were debt or equity investment instruments; the important concern was that more of the American currency was invested in American instruments. The by-product was growth in the financial markets, which in turn grew the American economy.

The fourth reason was that America eventually realized profits from the improved amounts of capital for investment. The real bonus was that this contributed to economic growth, domestically, in a reduced or inflation-free atmosphere. The fifth reason was sort of a residual effect. Since the use of U.S. dollars improved the eventual demand for them, since trading for petroleum was to be conducted with the use of those dollars, then the dollar would inevitably grow in strength on the international financial markets. Even though there was phenomenal currency depletion from the U.S. economy, since the currency was in use internationally, it would work to ameliorate any adverse effects secondary to the depletion of international trading accounts with other nations. The sixth and final reason was that a strong American currency would decrease the overall costs associated with petroleum purchases from nations such as Iraq. The reality was that the U.S. could print more purchasing power, a paper trade for the long run, in exchange for the trade in real services or goods, from other nations, in the short run (Looney, 2004).

The Exercise of the European Union's Trade Power in International Trade

The literature noted that the EU was the global leader, with regard to trading power. This allowed the individual institutions to foster better agreements, due to the nature of the size of the EU market and cumulative growth attributed to the EU's aggregate economy. Part of the stranglehold, of the European Union's negotiating strength, evolved from the fact that there was only one entity, the European Commission, which was empowered to negotiate agreements in the international trading system. The Commission shaped the economics associated with the spread of globalization because it was the sole determinant of the supply of wealth, services, and commodities that the member nations received or sold internationally in the trade arena. Thus, the EU not only used the mass marketing or purchasing, associated with economies of scale, but also was the arbiter of all trade disputes; not only among member nations, but also on behalf of those nations with the rest of the trading blocs in the international trade arena.

The European Union was shown to be in a position to ask for and obtain trading concessions, even from the United States, as well as from other national players in the international trade arena. It was reported that these trade strength assertions were not based upon a show of such strength, but they were predicated upon the imposition of trading solidarity, among the EU nations, to reject replication or a duplication of effort. The EU's Commission was shown to resort to the letter of the law, instead of free fall trading based upon whims or market caprice. In essence, the European Union did not show any examples of weakness propagated by any sort of trade reason, but they demonstrated a certain solidarity or uniformity of purpose to act as an economic unit; composed of the member nations. This was likened to the sort of loan conditionality enforced by the International Monetary Fund upon member nations.

The European Union's negotiating goal was the economic solidarity, as well as some strict language that described a supposedly open access to trade with the EU's member nations; provided such access was reinforced with packages to the member nations that included linking to reciprocal access to markets and aid for the individual nations. The EU's Commission was reported to be working toward the integration of the EU's nations and the promotion of globalization, and related interests, for all European Union member nations. Unfortunately, the spatial characteristics of the promotion of the EU's regionally-centered tendencies, and the promotion of its economic interests over non-EU nations, have drawn sharp criticism from global organizations, such as the WTO. The global trade organizations and interests have questioned whether the EU will really continue to support the development of multipartite international trade, without quietly fostering trade diversion at the expense of non-EU nations (Meunier and Nicolaidis, 2006).

The Five Wars of International Trade Resulting From the Spread of Globalization

Naim (2003) noted that the highest profile economic, international trade war was described as the war regarding illegal drugs. The value, purportedly advertised by the United Nations in the late 1990s, was alleged to be equivalent to the GDP of the country of Spain; close to one-half trillion dollars or about eight percent of the entire world's legitimate, international trade (annual value). The essential consideration was concluded to be that, even if the leaders of all of the drug cartels were imprisoned or killed, there was so much money involved, that there were people standing in line to assume those leadership positions, in the crime families and organizations, to continue the management of the illegal revenue stream.

The second of the five wars involved the movement and trade of illegal arms. The United Nations contended that about three percent of all small arms in use, in the world, were in use by legitimate law enforcement or government organizations; such as the police. About one-fifth of all arms international trade was illegal guns and it generated about one billion dollars annually for the crime cartels and organizations. Governments, due to the proliferation of such arms trades, and through organizational or government corruption, were demonstrated to be ineffective and basically without recourse in the apprehension or prosecution of these arms dealers who sell illegal arms on the international markets.

The third war was discussed to be the war of the sale of stolen intellectual property: music CDs; books; and items such as computer software. Although the other wars have some value for discussion, the revenue generated did not compare with the first three wars already discussed. The other minor illegal wars being waged on the international trade front were: "human organs;" "endangered species;" stolen art;" and "toxic waste" (pp. 30-32).

Influences on the European Union's External Trade Policy

The literature discussed the probable, potential influences that could affect the European Union's potential, external trade policy within the international trade arena. The framework of the principal and agent relationship was used to discuss various aspects of the trade policies to date, with regard to the bilateral versus the multilateral aspects associated with the levels of governing fiscal policy secondary to the 25 European Union's member nations. The relationships were interesting since the studies noted a variety of labels; the most important labels of which were the European Union Commission, and member governments, as agents and the Council of Ministers, and the public at large, as principals. The theoretical discussion centered upon the proposed abilities of the principals, with regard to their responsibilities and powers, with relation to agents, to: screen and select agents; control those agents in the conduct of duties; and to discipline and punish agents who acted inappropriately.

The largest problem, uncovered in the literature, was the democratic republics, who were members of the EU, which could not seem to properly manage the voting process to agree on the candidates or policies for enforcement. Unfortunately, this lack of direction was exacerbated by the press in all of the member nations that spared no expense or effort to condemn the ruling formulators for the smallest indiscretion or error. Failures and performance issues were punished by the electorate by simply failing to re-install the policymakers for another term. This was supported by empirical data that stemmed from frequent government official turnover.

There really were no information asymmetry issues, since the public had high-tech access to the daily workings of government and trade policy formulation. Unfortunately, the Council of Ministers does not meet publicly, which makes the body more difficult to control by the EU's member governments. However, due to disagreements over such transparency of reporting issues, the power of Parliaments in the various member nations has been increasing, in order to influence trade policy at different levels of formulation and institution. The EU could institute three particular types of international trade policy: agreements among different groups; economics and international trade treaties; and certain agreements that concerned trade, which came under the auspices of the Commission. Some of the increase in the parliamentary strength, of the various nations, could have stemmed from the fact that individual parliaments must still approve aggregate trade policy. The purpose behind the check and balance in the system was that institutional changes were generally necessary, secondary to the approval of those trade agreements, and parliaments were required to approve budgets for that sort of activity domestically. Further, the parliaments were required to note whether those trade agreements were within the limits allowed by domestic laws. Although the Commission and other group entities under the EU have major powers for international trade negotiation, the principal-agent relationship existed in the regional parts of nations to check the flight of that power out to the international trade arena (Reichert and Jungblut, 2007).

The Deep Trade Agenda, Trade Politics, and Market Integration of the European Union

The literature revealed that the European Union has not been as active on the obvious scene, in international trade, when considering the traditional issues associated with such trade. There has been a progressive shift to the investing and fiscal policy formulation aspects of trade before it reached the nation's borders. The newer trade participants, such as NGOs, groups that formerly had no interactions with trade, and governments, have made their voices heard in the negotiations concerning trading agreements and treaties. Developing countries have started to increase their demands, when trading with the United States and with the European Union.

The EU has responded with its own particular international trade agenda, or deep trade, in such that the member nations now were starting to seek multi-lateral trading platform agreements, instead of the antiquated unilateral or bilateral agreements from only several years earlier. These trade politics have reached the parliaments of the member nations and special interest groups have participated in the lobbying to a large extent. Part of the game plan advocated by special interests and the non-trade groups, was the position that the new trading conditionality, of the European Union's aggregate trading position, should allow market access predicated upon the potential trading government's domestic policy adjustments; or based upon present or future concessions involving the present trade agreements. Developing countries have observed this sort of trading action and have been wrangling to position themselves close to similar concessions from potential trading partner nations.

The balance of power has been shown to be involved in a gradual shift away from the developed nations, in the international trading arena, and has begun to accumulate in the hands of the wrangling, developing nations, since they have begun to act in concert on a variety of trade issues. This action has been observed in other global organizations, but wrangling has been the most obvious among member nations of the World Trade Organization. The European Union's policies regarding trade have been evolving to deal with this developing nation wrangling and, based upon recent experiences, as an integration marketing test, have come to center upon a countenance that was shown to exhibit four different phases of trade policy.

The first phase was the institution of types of policies that protected the EU's group interests, based upon the regulation of trade policy, from external unacceptable approaches from undesired, global traders. The second was the fostering of sanctions and other trade barriers as a unified front, when wrangling nations had excessively impeded the conduct of international trade. The third phase was the reduction of internal trade barriers, among EU member nations, to provide a unified front against non-member nations and border trade issues that could occur. The fourth phase was a predisposition for trade with nations that echoed the sentiments proposed by the EU member nations concerning certain requirements for concessions to labor and environmental issues. This stance was in keeping with the EU's platform to encourage the promotion of the plurality of trade agreements among member nations, trade liberalization, and the fostering of human rights (Young and Peterson, 2006).

Depth Summary

This literature review essay built upon the theoretical perspectives and critical analyses presented in the Breadth component of this paper by using those international trade theorists, and the applicable parts of their respective theories, as a foundation for the discussion involving the current research that was introduced in the annotations above. The integrated focus of the annotated research articles discussed above was international trade theory as it related to the development of international trade, national foreign policy, and the conduct of trade internationally among nations and to the development of a platform of values that is useful in international trade as it relates to international trade theory, national foreign policy, and the conduct of trade internationally among nations. The outline of the organization of this literature survey included major aspects of international trade theory and contemporary developments of specific concepts in international trade theory and how those concepts related to practical applications of international trade theory, national foreign policy, and the conduct of trade internationally among nations: international trade and the mechanics of statecraft; international trade structural linkages in treaty negotiations; international trade regulation as a response to export discrimination; intranational and international adjustments to liberalized, international trade; trade politics and foreign policy in multi-lateral international trade; trade liberalization and economic growth in developing countries; protectionism, restrictions, and barriers to contemporary international trade; mercantilist commercial policy and the regulation of international trade; classic, economic history, policy responses to international trade challenges; uses of economic statecraft to foster secondary state, international trade support; the use of U.S. dollars as the international currency for oil, international trade; the exercise of the European Union's trade power in international trade; the five wars of international trade resulting from the spread of globalization; influences on the European Union's external trade policy; and the Deep Trade Agenda, trade politics, and market integration of the European Union.

The rationale of the Depth narrative was to explore in detail these fifteen named aspects of international trade theory, and contemporary developments of specific concepts in international trade theory, and how those concepts related to practical applications of international trade theory, national foreign policy, and the conduct of trade internationally among nations. Analysis of the various contemporary developments of the specific concepts in international trade theory and how those concepts related to practical applications of international trade theory, national foreign policy, and the conduct of trade internationally, was provided with relation to the theories espoused in the Breadth segment, to improve the reader's understanding of these subjects and to provide a foundation for analysis, comparison, and contrast in the Application segment of this paper.

APPLICATION

APPLIED INTERNATIONAL TRADE

Introduction

The Application demonstration project is comprised of the development of a theoretical, overall structure of a *stand-alone* presentation that could be used in a specific application to conduct briefing symposia for "C-class" corporate officers who help to conduct international trade on behalf of multi-national corporations. The Application component also consists of a scholarly essay of about 10 pages and critically evaluates this theoretical presentation of some 25 pages of slides and notes in light of the theories from the Breadth and the research from the Depth. The 25 page presentation is located in Appendix 1 at the conclusion of this demonstration.

The contemporary, constructive, social change purpose of this application construct is the prospective enlightenment of corporate "C-class" officers so that these officers are more aware of the constructive choices available for international trade. These officers will then be better informed to effectively conduct such trade in order to promote global "win-win" trading among nations.

Application Essay

Trade Mission Structure and Corporate Performance

Beeman, Rosebrock, and Tran (2007) demonstrated that the increases in jobs fostered by exports and microeconomic organizations, which were designated as *for profit* or otherwise, have instituted a variety of benefit-driven sessions that trained companies to improve the creation of those exports. Some of the literature was skeptical concerning the value of such programs and whether those programs actually promoted increases in job creation, goods exportation, or aspects of company growth. There was a growing body of literature that discussed some related implications of "firm performance, exporting, firm characteristics, and export assistance programs" (p. 41).

The literature has demonstrated a variety of results, from firms that exported being shown to be in a faster growth mode compared to firms that had higher job creation numbers; but their output suffered. The literature also demonstrated that the size of the firm did not have a relationship to the volume of exports. An investigation of modestly sized Italian firms, over 4,000 firms in all, was shown to have some relationship demonstrated between a small firm and the volume of exports recorded. Some researchers have uncovered a correlation between export output and an increase in firm size; in overseas countries. Beeman,

Rosebrock, and Tran (2007) noted that First Energy, a trade promotion firm that worked through trade missions, during the time period from 1995 to 2004, helped "180 companies increase international sales by an estimated aggregate of $50 million to $117.6 million, following their participation in a trade mission/event. These results have been officially recognized at the state and national levels" (p. 43). The FE program aided medium-sized, or smaller companies that engaged in manufacturing, with exports to other North American neighbors, such as Canada and Mexico. The program has also been beneficial through aid provided to larger companies, but in the respect considering the marketing of services to the North American neighbors. The study, leading to the creation of the FE program, was instituted as the result of the study of empirical jobs data (Beeman, Rosebrock, and Tran, 2007).

Trade Barriers, Capital Flows, Globalization, and Politics in International Trade

The literature suggested that there were profound changes that had occurred in the aggregate world economy concerning national fiscal policy formulation. Trade barriers have been diminishing in concert with the increased flows of: market good and services through foreign exchanges; direct investment of foreign nations and companies; and the avalanche of capital through financial portfolios. The earnings in the world's developing nations have risen, which has created more and increasingly diverse markets for consumer goods and services, and there has been a rise in the interest, demonstrated by the public and the scholarly community, in the areas of political policies and the aspects associated with globalization. The literature demonstrated evidence of the position that it was formerly believed that countries, secondary to the advent of globalization, experienced decreased market strength and trade decision-making.

If one were to explain the phenomena associated with these observations through regional trade, then regional politics and trading agreements need to be examined, such as the aspects of trade and regulation secondary to NAFTA. If globalization and these changes were examined, then general trade theory (Heckscher-Ohlin model) or the Ricardian theory's position on comparative advantage, along with the aspects, such as transport conditions and communication upgrades, need to be studied. Some studies indicated that the growth increases occurring in developed countries, over the previous two decades, was attributable to manufacturing services' use, instead of the amount of the segment of GDP that was traded in the global markets. Although Ricardian comparative advantage helped, it was not the total answer.

Some studies noted that stakeholders that participated in the factors of production, would eventually experience forecastable changes in wealth based upon trade openness or protectionist trade sanctions. Nations that had surplus capital would be characterized by industrialists that supported trade openness and workers that sought to restrict it. There was a minority that saw the factors of production as tied to specific industries, and that those factors were not mobile to other industries. Governments were demonstrated to restrict imports during economic downturns and stop capital from leaving the country; to pursue foreign, rates of interest that were more competitive. Unfortunately, nations in the EU, or those that have linked their currency to the U.S. dollar, Hong Kong for instance, have severely reduced their ability to formulate remedial, fiscal policies. It was suggested that globalization was intended to promote the ease of foreign capital movement to firms that required capital inflows to produce domestically. Unfortunately, since international capital markets have been increasingly required to provide more and more remedial sustenance for trade and business, there has been expressed a concern that trade openness has progressed to the point where the institutions that have buffered international trade for decades may no longer be able to support the current international market structure (Berger, 2000).

International Trade Between Southern States and Latin America

The literature noted that municipal, state, and federal fiscal policies, in the United States, have addressed the emerging trends of international trade as an integral part of the developing structure of aggregate economics. The policy formulators acknowledged that this global trade influenced and promoted the marketing of goods and the creation of jobs and a number of companies have realized that explosive marketing associated with exports was a potential solution to the search for new sales channels, improvement to the variety of those channels, and increases net profits. However, only the top four-dozen American trading partners have acknowledged such opportunities for growth and sales. Of the global trading partners, the Latin American countries have been instrumental as trading partners with the American southern states region. The growth of trading volume with the United States, considering one-dozen Latin American countries, has increased more than two-dozen fold in the last decade. The statistics have demonstrated that trade, according to the United States' GDP figures, compared with the one-dozen Latin American countries, posted gains of over 200 percent in the two decades ending with the turn of the millennium.

The trade between the American southern states and Latin America has not yet reached its potential. During the previous decade, the southern states' export figures exhibited more than a 250 percent increase. This staggering growth figure was far in excess of the export trade associated with the 50 principal trading partners that trade with the U.S. At the beginning of the Clinton Administration, one-third of all exports, of all exports of the southern states, were composed of trade to the one-dozen Latin American nations. At the turn of the millennium, the figure approached almost 40 percent. This trade with Latin America continues to grow and has improved job creation, increased the creation of intellectual property, created remedial income, and has improved standards for southern states citizens. Part of the growth, particularly in the Carolinas, Texas, and Florida, has resulted from the foreign trade bonds and trading with foreign nations secondary to brotherly linked cities between those states and foreign nations.

The fiscal policies associated with the international trade, developed by all levels of government in the U.S. have contributed tremendously to the creation and growth of international trade and have taken advantage of new markets globally; particularly Latin American nations as trading partners. Some of the tools that were utilized, to set the proper tone to encourage such trading, were: allowances in the taxation structures, which attracted direct, foreign investment; structural changes in the local environment to induce, reward and retain the investments; the inception, promotion and participation in trade delegations, whose mission it was to improve exports to the foreign nations; and the training of the business leaders that participated in the trade delegations and businesses created and fostered to engage in such foreign trade (CanagaRetna, 2002).

The Decline of National Sovereignty With Relation to International Trade

International trade, and relations for the past 350 years, has supported the underlying concept that nations had the autonomy to conduct their own affairs, concerning their own domestic and international affairs, in whatever manner the national government wished. The literature suggested, over the next three decades, that this concept will gradually wane and then, essentially, vanish. The sovereignty mantle will then be assumed by entities, other than nations, such as: NGOs; multi-national corporations; and international or regional types of microeconomic organizations and institutions. These institutions and organizations will deal with issues such as: military material; intellectual property; labor; capital; means of production; and commodities used as factors for production. This concept redirects a main concern associated with the concept of national sovereignty: the management of everything that moves over, around, or under a nation's boundaries. The real concern for a country will eventually be not what other nations can do to a country on homeland soil, but how subject that nation will be to global forces and movement that would be beyond the ken of homeland security and fiscal policy.

The literature suggested that domestic parliaments, which would not provide the necessities for their citizenry, would risk the ultimate loss of all autonomy. Homeland security issues could arise, secondary to this sort of governmental apathy, which could destabilize a nation and encourage massive inflows of itinerant labor. This would then provide the inroads necessary for other ills, associated with globalization, to enter nations unchecked. This was addressed in Naim (2003). It was surmised that states that sponsor terrorist organizations, or the factors associated with such activity, would then have opened their borders for the results of those eventual attacks to be focused upon their own homeland without reprieve.

The studies noted that a 21st century goal could be the creation of advanced, national policies that would thwart the non-sovereign interests from gaining even a preliminary foothold within a nation's borders, as well as some disciplinary mechanism to deal with malicious organizations that do attempt such incursions. The most prevalent indication of these types of incursions has to do with the conduct of international trade. Even though certain decrees from the WTO do decrease a nation's sovereignty, the nations have generally agreed because, in the short run, economic benefits have been realized by each nation in question's citizenry. When the developed nations increase their acceptance of these international rulings, from NGOs and other sources, much of the structure will have been erected to fulfill the prophecy of non-sovereign entities controlling the nature and nurture of international politics and world trade. This will then put in place the concern that autonomous states should be concerned with, instead of what states could do to one another as sovereign entities, what global organizations could do to the states and what policies a government could enforce upon its own citizenry (Haass, 2005).

Implications for International Trade and Integration Resulting from Globalization

The literature indicated that the issues, concerning globalization, were debated among decision-makers, and that the public was generally in favor of the results associated with economic globalization; however, the public only accepted those results with trepidation and caution. It was shown that the public believed that direct foreign investment and international trade would improve conditions in the nations examined, which included some of the most destitute nations; namely sub-Saharan Africa. In sharp contrast, the public in developed nations, such as the U.S. and the EU have shown diminished signs of the acceptance of globalization's economic benefits. One reason, for the increasing rejection of globalization's effects, by the people of developed nations, was that the citizenry were concerned about adverse effects to the environment. However, the general attitude, concerning the market availability, pervasion of MNCs, and global trade, as demonstrated by almost 50 countries, was that globalization's effects have been embraced.

The literature noted that the destitute nations' labor has contributed to social unrest, associated with labor movement in the destitute countries, and that the labor has moved into the cities for job searches, whereas developed nations' workers have noted that jobs have re-appeared in foreign nations. Groups in the almost 50 nations surveyed, indicated that the growth of international trade has had positive economic growth input to their domestic economies. The organization that has helped to foster positive public opinion, concerning the advantages of globalization, was confirmed to be multi-national corporations. Over 80 percent, of the almost 50 countries surveyed, indicated that multi-national corporations had contributed growth to their national economies. Unfortunately, the negative results stemmed from surveys taken in nations of the Middle East, or from developing nations with weaker economies.

Other survey results showed that the western views of implemented capitalism were beneficial to global economies, even in spite of mixed results in some nations. Market openness has had positive, surveyed results in more than half of three-dozen developed nations surveyed, over the past five years. Latin American countries have also indicated, by survey, that the rise of capitalism was welcomed to their respective economies. Surveyed results indicated that the poorer nations were concerned about the less than admirable globalization qualities of lost rituals, unequal job opportunities, and issues with growth that adversely affected the environment. The developing nations noted that market openness and international trade would increase aggregate economic output and that growth would not be evenly distributed among the members of the domestic economies (Kohut and Wike, 2008).

Economic Development and Multinational Corporations

The literature indicated that the concept of the multinational corporation, with respect to international trade and international relations, arose some time after the end of

World War Two. MNCs have come to be integral participants in the global economy. Studies have indicated that, with regard to theories of dependency, microeconomic institutions in the domestic economy become dependent upon direct foreign investment. The nation of Singapore, which was not subject to international trade in the conventional sense, adopted the host nation stance, since it was bereft of natural resources for production, in order to entice MNCs to conduct trade within and through the borders of Singapore. MNCs saw this invitation and brought foreign investment that more directly linked the economy of Singapore to the rest of global trade. It was interesting to note that the domestic government of Singapore fostered these tendencies, instead of the MNCs that could have, but didn't; similar to MNC conduct in other developing nations throughout the world's markets.

Ricardian theory espoused the idea that there were nations that could not produce every good or service that was required in their domestic economy. The global market eliminated duplication of effort and the use of resources so that the discussed effort and resources could be applied elsewhere. Technological advances and increased foreign capital, introduced to host nations, tended to improve the host nation's domestic economy. Part of the current thought associated with this theory, was the fact that developed nations would advance, at the expense of developing nations, since MNCs were viewed as the purveyors of global capital reserves. The studies noted that operational risk was the result of host nation changes in revenues, results, or the daily business activities that affected the MNCs. The idea of risk was also affected by the host nation's fiscal policies, the development of infrastructure for trade, and the domestic government's reliability. Researchers indicated that the Asian Tigers have virtually no enterprise requirements to open business, but that countries in the Middle East were extremely restrictive of new businesses, requiring dozens of times the national income, per person, just to open a business.

Thus, it was noted that the government's requirements for businesses were the greatest causes of failure in the domestic economy. Singapore's economy grew quickly due to the reduced requirements for direct investment, thus promoting capital movements, and the diminished barriers to international trade; there was a dearth of sanctions and trade requirements.

While England was an economic contributor, in Singapore, the British government decided against the formal education of the public and set no goals or plans for that education. However, economically, certain industries were encouraged: computer development; vehicle manufacturing; and electronics. The Economic Expansion Incentive Act (1967) was instituted to foster economic growth and foreign investment. As a result, MNCs started to directly invest and grow the economy in Singapore. Since operational and investment risk had been reduced, the Singapore government improved trade by building infrastructure, with regard to better transportation; this reduced transportation costs and improved the ease of trade. While the infrastructure was developed, manufacturing was integral to the development of revenue. MNCs, in exchange for developing the nation of Singapore's economy, were rewarded with improved labor and packages of trade incentives, reduced regulation of trade, better trade infrastructure, and a solid, local government (Nizamuddin, 2007).

Trade Promotion Through the Use of the International Organization for Standardization

The literature promoted the twofold use of the ISO standards to improve the conduct of international trade: the economic labeling of goods, or services agreements, could diminish domestic importation barriers to trade; and examination of the useful product's cycle could prevent environmental issues associated with importation of goods and services. Studies demonstrated that incentives, such as those given for products that protected the environment or for global markets that fostered environmental goals, were constructive and beneficial. There has been some work, on the part of firms, to voluntarily work in an environmentally friendly manner.   However, there were limitations to use of ISO standards, with regard to the environment and trade barriers.

ISO standards were originally instituted for the benefit of certain industries. A side benefit, for consumers and distributors, has been certification of the actual standards, but through a disinterested third party. The third party, also a non-essential requirement, has had the tendency to encourage consistency of products and services. The newer ISO standards, which address impact upon the environment, have addressed something that has already been regulated by many countries around the world. Thus, since this was something that was already regulated, the relationship between government policies and the standards themselves was a tenuous one.

In order to achieve the variety of different ISO ratings, the products and the processes must be determined to be standardized, to produce uniformity and reliability. In order to obtain such ratings, the requirements were mandatory, although seeking such ratings was still voluntary. This was one of the admirable processes, the ISO standardizations, which has occurred secondary to globalization. This overall standardization process has provided some relief to governments for oversight and increased regulation, and has improved the access to global markets for MNCs by opening access to global markets with easier transactions (Wirth, 2009).

Application Summary

The Application demonstration project was comprised of the development of a theoretical, overall structure of a *stand-alone* presentation that could be used in a specific application to conduct briefing symposia for "C-class" corporate officers who help to conduct international trade on behalf of multi-national corporations. The Application component consists of a scholarly essay of about 10 pages and critically evaluates this theoretical presentation of some 25 pages of slides and notes in light of the theories from the Breadth and the research from the Depth.

The contemporary, constructive, social change purpose of this application construct is the prospective enlightenment of corporate "C-class" officers so that these officers are more aware of the constructive choices available for international trade. These officers will then be better informed to effectively conduct such trade in order to promote global "win-win" trading among nations.

References

Afilalo, A. & Patterson, D. (2006). Statecraft, trade and the order of states. *Chicago Journal of International Law, 6*(2), 725-759. Retrieved January 8, 2009, from Research Library database. (Document ID: 1011292111).

Beeman, D., Rosebrock, H., & Tran, O. (2007). Do structured international trade missions improve corporate performance? *Economic Development Journal, 6*(3), 41-48. Retrieved from ABI/INFORM Global. (Document ID: 1550277901).

Berger, S. (2000). Globalization and politics. *Annual Review of Political Science, 3*(1), 43-62.

CanagaRetna, S. (2002). International trade between Latin America and the southern legislative conference states. *Spectrum: The Journal of State Government, Winter Edition,* 20-21. Article summary republished from Forging New Trade Relationships: Latin America and the Southern Legislative Conference States, originally published in July 2001.

Crump, L. (2006). Competitively-linked and non-competitively-linked negotiations: Bilateral *trade policy* negotiations in Australia, Singapore and the United States. *International Negotiation, 11*(3), 431-466. Retrieved

January 8, 2009, from Academic Search Premier database. (Accession Number: 23457141).

Dur, A. (2007). Foreign discrimination, protection for exporters, and U.S. *Trade* liberalization. *International Studies Quarterly, 51*(2), 457-480. Retrieved January 8, 2009, from Academic Search Premier database. (Accession Number: 25558864).

Faber, B. (2007). Towards the spatial patterns of sectoral adjustments to *trade* liberalisation: The case of NAFTA in Mexico. *Growth and Change, 38*(4), 567-594. Retrieved January 8, 2009, from Academic Search Premier database. (Accession Number: 27648211).

Haass, R. (2005). Sovereignty. *Foreign Policy,*(150), 54-55. Retrieved from ABI/INFORM Global. (Document ID: 888792291).

Heckscher, E. (1922). *The continental system*. Clarendon Press: London, England.

Heckscher, E., & Ohlin, B. ([1919], [1924], 1991). *Heckscher-Ohlin trade theory*. MIT Press: London, England.

Helpman, E., & Krugman, P. (1985). *Market structure and foreign trade*. The MIT Press: London, England.

Hurrell, A., & Narlikar, A. (2006). A new politics of confrontation? Brazil and India in multilateral *trade* negotiations. *Global Society: Journal of Interdisciplinary International Relations, 20*(4), 415-433. Retrieved January 8, 2009, from Academic Search Premier database (Accession Number: 22908970).

Isard, W. (Ed.). ([1956], 1972). *Location and space-economy*. The MIT Press: London, England.

Kneller, R. (2007). No miracles here: *Trade policy*, fiscal *policy* and economic growth. *Journal of Development Studies, 43*(7), 1248-1269. Retrieved January 8, 2009, from Academic Search Premier database. (Accession Number: 26952164).

Kohut, A., & Wike, R. (2008). Assessing globalization: Benefits and drawbacks of trade and integration. *Harvard International Review, 30*(1), 70-74. Retrieved from ABI/INFORM Global. (Document ID: 1504550061).

Krugman, P., & Obstfeld, M. (2006). *International economics: Theory & policy* (7th ed.). New York: Pearson, Addison/Wesley.

Lavin, F. (2008). The social dimension of **trade**: The village blacksmith paradox. *Brown Journal of World Affairs, 14*(2), 241-251. Retrieved January 8, 2009, from Academic Search Premier database. (Accession Number: 32819055).

Leng, T. (2005). Commercial conflict and regulation in the discourse of trade in seventeenth-century England. *The Historical Journal, 48*(4), 933-954. Retrieved January 8, 2009, from Research Library database. (Document ID: 986982451).

Looney, R. (2004). Petroeuros: A threat to U.S. interests in the gulf? *Middle East Policy, 11*(1), 26-37. Retrieved January 8, 2009, from Research Library database. (Document ID: 611327931).

Lobell, S. (2004). Historical lessons to extend America's great power tenure. *World Affairs, 166*(4), 175-184. Retrieved January 8, 2009, from Research Library database. (Document ID: 597812861).

Lobell, S. (2008). The second face of American security: The US-Jordan free trade agreement as security policy.

Comparative Strategy, 27(1), 88-100. Retrieved January 8, 2009, from Academic Search Premier database. (Accession Number: 31168067).

Meunier, S. & Nicolaidis, K. (2006). The European Union as a conflicted trade power. *Journal of European Public Policy, 13*(6), 906-925. Retrieved January 8, 2009, from Academic Search Premier database. (Accession Number: 21806746).

Naim, M. (2003). The five wars of globalization. *Foreign Policy, 134*(1), 28-36. Retrieved January 8, 2009, from ABI/INFORM Global database. (Document ID: 278453641).

Nizamuddin, A. (2007). Multinational corporations and economic development: The lessons of Singapore. *International Social Science Review, 82*(3 & 4), 149-162.

Ohlin, B. ([1933], 1952). *Interregional and international trade.* Harvard University Press: Cambridge, MA.

Reichert, M., & Jungblut, B. (2007). European Union external *trade policy*: Multilevel principal–agent relationships. *Policy Studies Journal, 35*(3), 395-418. Retrieved January 8, 2009, from Academic Search Premier database. (Accession Number: 27230504).

Ricardo, D. ([1817], 2004). *The principles of political economy and taxation.* New York: Dover.

Wirth, D. (2009). The international organization for standardization: Private voluntary standards as swords and shields. *Boston College Environmental Affairs Law Review, 36*(1), 79-102. Retrieved from Academic Search Premier. (AN 37181941).

Young, A., & Peterson, J. (2006). The EU and the new *trade politics*. *Journal of European Public Policy, 13*(6), 795-814. Retrieved January 8, 2009, from Academic Search Premier database. (Accession Number: 21806745).

APPENDIX 1

Corporate Officer's Symposium for International Trade

A Theoretical, Briefing Symposium for Corporate Officers, of Multinational Corporations, Who Manage and Conduct International Trade - *For the improvement of trade conduct, through informed choices, for global "win-win" trading among nations and in global markets.*

Title Slide

Introduction

- This compliancy symposium was created in order to foster a greater cooperation among international trading professionals.
- The purpose of this symposium presentation is to acquaint trade professionals, and corporate officers, with the new research concerning the contemporary issues associated with international trade.

Slide 2

Summary of Topics to be Presented

- *Trade Mission Structure and Corporate Performance*
- *Trade Barriers, Capital Flows, Globalization, and Politics in International Trade*
- *International Trade Between Southern States and Latin America*
- *The Decline of National Sovereignty With Relation to International Trade*
- *Implications for International Trade and Integration Resulting from Globalization*
- *Economic Development and Multinational Corporations*
- *Trade Promotion Through the Use of the International Organization for Standardization*

Slide 3

Mission Structure Trade and Corporate Performance

- Job increases secondary to exports
- Microeconomic organizations create jobs
- Company training sessions promote jobs
- Do trade programs really create jobs?

Slide 4 - SPEAKER'S NOTES

Trade Mission Structure and Corporate Performance

Beeman, Rosebrock, and Tran (2007) demonstrated that the increases in jobs fostered by exports and microeconomic organizations, which were designated as for profit or otherwise, have instituted a variety of benefit-driven sessions that trained companies to improve the creation of those exports.

Some of the literature was skeptical concerning the value of such programs and whether those programs actually promoted increases in job creation, goods exportation, or aspects of company growth.

Trade Mission Structure and Corporate Performance (continued)

- Research literature addressed issues
- Programs related to performance
- Trade promotion firms do increase sales
- Trade missions promote more revenue

Slide 5 - SPEAKER'S NOTES

There was a growing body of literature that discussed some related implications of firm performance, exporting, firm characteristics, and export assistance programs.

Beeman, Rosebrock, and Tran (2007) noted that First Energy, a trade promotion firm that worked through trade missions, during the time period from 1995 to 2004, helped 180 companies increase international sales by an estimated aggregate of $50 million to $117.6 million, following their participation in a trade mission/event.

Trade Mission Structure and Corporate Performance (continued)

- Trade program aided smaller to medium companies
- Manufacturers received exports aid
- Improved North American trade to neighbors
- Trade program created from study of jobs data

Slide 6 - SPEAKER'S NOTES

The FE program aided medium-sized or smaller companies that engaged in manufacturing, with exports to other North American neighbors, such as Canada and Mexico.

The study, leading to the creation of the FE program, was instituted as the result of the study of empirical jobs data (Beeman, Rosebrock, and Tran, 2007).

Trade Barriers, Capital Flows, Globalization, and Politics in International Trade

- Trade barriers have gradually dropped
- Goods and services flowing in exchanges
- Direct investment and capital flows are up
- Developing nations' earnings have risen

Slide 7 - SPEAKER'S NOTES

Trade Barriers, Capital Flows, Globalization, and Politics in International Trade

Trade barriers have been diminishing in concert with the increased flows of: market goods and services through foreign exchanges; direct investment of foreign nations and companies; and the avalanche of capital through financial portfolios.

The earnings, in the world's developing nations, have risen, which has created more and increasingly diverse markets for consumer goods and services, and there has been a rise in the interest, demonstrated by the public and the scholarly community, in the areas of political policies and the aspects associated with globalization.

Trade Barriers, Capital Flows, Globalization, and Politics in International Trade (continued)

- Trade myths have been debunked
- Research shows globalization increased markets
- Research shows globalization improved decisions
- Stakeholder wealth increased from trade

Slide 8 - SPEAKER'S NOTES

The literature demonstrated evidence of the position that it was formerly believed that countries, secondary to the advent of globalization, experienced decreased market strength and trade decision-making.

Some studies noted that stakeholders that participated in the factors of production, would eventually experience forecastable changes in wealth based upon trade openness or protectionist trade sanctions.

Trade Barriers, Capital Flows, Globalization, and Politics in International Trade (continued)

- Factors of production not always mobile
- Governments restrict imports during downturns
- Governments can stop capital - foreign investment
- Globalization was intended to ease capital moves

Slide 9 - SPEAKER'S NOTES

There was a minority that saw the factors of production as tied to specific industries, and that those factors were not mobile to other industries. Governments were demonstrated to restrict imports during economic downturns and stop capital from leaving the country; to pursue foreign, rates of interest that were more competitive.

It was suggested that globalization was intended to promote the ease of foreign capital movement to firms that required capital inflows to produce domestically.

International Trade Between Southern States and Latin America

- Levels of government policies address trade
- International trade is part of economic structure
- Global trade influenced sales of goods/ services
- Latin America has become important trade partner

Slide 10 - SPEAKER'S NOTES

International Trade Between Southern States and Latin America

The literature noted that municipal, state, and federal fiscal policies, in the United States, have addressed the emerging trends of international trade as an integral part of the developing structure of aggregate economics.

The policy formulators acknowledged that this global trade influenced and promoted the marketing of goods and the creation of jobs and a number of companies have realized that explosive marketing associated with exports was a potential solution to the search for new sales channels, improvement to the variety of those channels, and to increases in net profits.

Of the global trading partners, the Latin American countries have been instrumental as trading partners with the American southern states region.

International Trade Between Southern States and Latin America (continued)

- U.S. trading volume has been increasing in general
- U.S. trade has increased with Latin America
- One-dozen Latin American countries improved GDP
- U.S./Latin American trade was up over 200 %

Slide 11 - SPEAKER'S NOTES

The growth of trading volume with the United States, considering one-dozen Latin American countries, has increased more than two-dozen fold in the last decade.

The statistics have demonstrated that trade, according to the United States' GDP figures, compared with the one-dozen Latin American countries, has posted gains of over 200 percent in the two decades ending with the turn of the millennium.

International Trade Between Southern States and Latin America
(continued)

- Trade growth in Texas, Carolinas, and Florida
- Linked cities promoted foreign trade increases
- Governments used tools and incentives for trade
- Trade delegations and businesses worked together

Slide 12 - SPEAKER'S NOTES

Part of the growth, particularly in the Carolinas, Texas, and Florida, has resulted from the foreign trade bonds and trading with foreign nations secondary to brotherly linked cities between those states and foreign nations.

Some of the tools that were utilized, to set the proper tone to encourage such trading, were: allowances in the taxation structures, which attracted direct, foreign investment; structural changes in the local environment to induce, reward and retain the investments; the inception, promotion and participation in trade delegations, whose mission it was to improve exports to the foreign nations; and the training of the business leaders that participated in the trade delegations and businesses created and fostered to engage in such foreign trade (CanagaRetna, 2002).

The Decline of National Sovereignty With Relation to International Trade

- Trade supported centuries of national sovereignty
- Sovereignty now being assumed by organizations
- Will nations still enjoy sovereignty in the future?
- Will global forces dictate fiscal policy and trade?

Slide 13 - SPEAKER'S NOTES

International trade, and relations for the past 350 years, has supported the underlying concept that nations had the autonomy to conduct their own affairs, concerning their own domestic and international affairs, in whatever manner the national government wished.

The sovereignty mantle will then be assumed by entities, other than nations, such as: NGOs; multi-national corporations; and international or regional types of microeconomic organizations and institutions.

The real concern for a country will eventually be not what other nations can do to a country on homeland soil, but how subject that nation will be to global forces and movement that would be beyond the ken of homeland security and fiscal policy.

The Decline of National Sovereignty With Relation to International Trade (continued)

- National parliaments at risk for loss of autonomy
- Homeland security risks could destabilize nations
- Globalization ills could enter nations unchecked
- New policies must deter non-sovereign interests

Slide 14 - SPEAKER'S NOTES

The literature suggested that domestic parliaments, which would not provide the necessities for their citizenry, would risk the ultimate loss of all autonomy.

Homeland security issues could arise, secondary to this sort of governmental apathy, which could destabilize a nation and encourage massive inflows of itinerant labor.

This would then provide the inroads necessary for other ills, associated with globalization, to enter nations unchecked.

The studies noted that a 21st century goal could be the creation of advanced, national policies that would thwart the non-sovereign interests from gaining even a preliminary foothold within a nation's borders, as well as some disciplinary mechanism to deal with malicious organizations that do attempt such incursions.

Implications for International Trade and Integration Resulting from Globalization

- Public was found to be in favor of globalization
- Public also cautious about effects of globalization
- Public believed trade/investment was improvement
- Developed nation's citizens - incomplete approval

Slide 15 - SPEAKER'S NOTES

Implications for International Trade and Integration Resulting from Globalization

The literature indicated that the issues, concerning globalization, were debated among decision-makers, and that the public was generally in favor of the results associated with economic globalization; however, the public only accepted those results with trepidation and caution.

It was shown that the public believed that direct foreign investment and international trade would improve conditions in the nations examined, which included some of the most destitute nations; namely sub-Saharan Africa.

In sharp contrast, the public in developed nations, such as the U.S. and in the EU, have shown diminished signs of the acceptance of globalization's economic benefits.

Implications for International Trade and Integration Resulting from Globalization (continued)

- Some have rejected globalization's effects
- Developed nations concerned about environment
- Poor nations' labor has contributed to unrest
- Developed nations' jobs have moved overseas

Slide 16 - SPEAKER'S NOTES

One reason, for the increasing rejection of globalization's effects, by the people of developed nations, was that the citizenry were concerned about the adverse effects to the environment.

The literature noted that the destitute nations' labor has contributed to social unrest, associated with labor movement in the destitute countries, and that the labor has moved into the cities for job searches, whereas developed nations' workers have noted that jobs have re-appeared in foreign nations.

Implications for International Trade and Integration Resulting from Globalization (continued)

- Almost 50 nations were surveyed
- Global trade created positive, economic growth
- Implementation of capitalism promoted trade
- Results of trade tended to vary by nation studied

Slide 17 - SPEAKER'S NOTES

Groups in the almost 50 nations surveyed, indicated that the growth of international trade has had positive economic growth input to their domestic economies.

Other survey results showed that the western views of implemented capitalism were beneficial to global economies, even in spite of mixed results in some nations.

Economic Development and Multinational Corporations

- Concept of the multinational corporation was new
- MNCs started to gain prominence after WW II
- Theories of dependency were examined
- Domestic institutions depend upon foreign capital

Slide 18 - SPEAKER'S NOTES

Economic Development and Multinational Corporations

The literature indicated that the concept of the multinational corporation, with respect to international trade and international relations, arose some time after the end of World War Two.
Studies have indicated that, with regard to theories of dependency, microeconomic institutions in the domestic economy become dependent upon direct foreign investment.

Economic Development and Multinational Corporations (continued)

- Singapore was originally apart from global trade
- For growth, Singapore adopted *host nation* stance
- Government promoted trade, instead of MNCs
- Operational risk reduced due to host nation policies

Slide 19 - SPEAKER'S NOTES

The nation of Singapore, which was not subject to international trade in the conventional sense, adopted the host nation stance, since it was bereft of natural resources for production, in order to entice MNCs to conduct trade within and through the borders of Singapore.

It was interesting to note that the domestic government of Singapore fostered these tendencies, instead of the MNCs that could have, but didn't; similar to MNC conduct in other developing nations throughout the world's markets.

The studies noted that operational risk, or the lack of it, was the result of host nation changes in revenues, results, or the daily business activities that affected the MNCs.

Economic Development and Multinational Corporations (continued)

- Risk was affected by the host nation's policies
- Risk reduced by infrastructure development
- British government did not develop local culture
- Key industries encouraged for economic growth

Slide 20 - SPEAKER'S NOTES

The idea of risk was also affected by the host nation's fiscal policies, the development of infrastructure for trade, and the domestic government's reliability.

While England was an economic contributor, in Singapore, the British government decided against the formal education of the public and set no goals or plans for that education.

However, economically, certain industries were encouraged: computer development; vehicle manufacturing; and electronics.

Economic Development and Multinational Corporations (continued)

- Economic regulation fostered growth/ investment
- Reduced risk promoted government improvements
- Improvements reduced costs and improved trade
- MNC development rewarded with labor and trade

Slide 21 - SPEAKER'S NOTES

The Economic Expansion Incentive Act (1967) was instituted to foster economic growth and foreign investment.

Since operational and investment risk had been reduced, the Singapore government improved trade by building infrastructure, with regard to better transportation; this reduced transportation costs and improved the ease of trade.

MNCs, in exchange for developing the nation of Singapore's economy, were rewarded with improved labor and packages of trade incentives, reduced regulation of trade, better trade infrastructure, and a solid, local government (Nizamuddin, 2007).

Trade Promotion Through the Use of the International Organization for Standardization

- Two main uses for ISO standards in global trade
- Reduce domestic trade barriers/help environment
- Environmental incentives constructive/ beneficial
- ISO standards competed with government policies

Slide 22 - SPEAKER'S NOTES

Trade Promotion Through the Use of the International Organization for Standardization

The literature promoted the twofold use of the ISO standards to improve the conduct of international trade: the economic labeling of goods, or services agreements, could diminish domestic importation barriers to trade; and examination of the useful product's cycle could prevent environmental issues associated with importation of goods and services. Studies demonstrated that incentives, such as those given for products that protected the environment or for global markets that fostered environmental goals, were constructive and beneficial.

The newer ISO standards, which addressed the impact upon the environment, have addressed something that has already been regulated by many countries around the world.

Trade Promotion Through the Use of the International Organization for Standardization (continued)

- Standardized products promoted uniformity
- Standardized products promoted reliability
- ISO standards occurred from globalization
- ISO reduces regulation/improves global trade

Slide 23 - SPEAKER'S NOTES

In order to achieve the variety of different ISO ratings, the products and the processes must be determined to be standardized, to produce uniformity and reliability.

This was one of the admirable processes, the ISO standardizations, which has occurred secondary to globalization.

This overall standardization process has provided some relief to governments for oversight and increased regulation, and has improved the access to global markets for MNCs by opening access to global markets with easier transactions (Wirth, 2009).

Summary of Topics Presented

- *Trade Mission Structure and Corporate Performance*
- *Trade Barriers, Capital Flows, Globalization, and Politics in International Trade*
- *International Trade Between Southern States and Latin America*
- *The Decline of National Sovereignty With Relation to International Trade*
- *Implications for International Trade and Integration Resulting from Globalization*
- *Economic Development and Multinational Corporations*
- *Trade Promotion Through the Use of the International Organization for Standardization*

Slide 24

REFERENCES

Beeman, D., Rosebrock, H., & Tran, O. (2007). Do structured international trade missions improve corporate performance? *Economic Development Journal, 6*(3), 41-48. Retrieved from ABI/INFORM Global. (Document ID: 1550277901).

Berger, S. (2000). Globalization and politics. *Annual Review of Political Science, 3*(1), 43-62.

CanagaRetna, S. (2002). International trade between Latin America and the southern legislative conference states. *Spectrum: The Journal of State Government, Winter Edition,* 20-21. Article summary republished from Forging New Trade Relationships: Latin America and the Southern Legislative Conference States, originally published in July 2001.

Haass, R. (2005). Sovereignty. *Foreign Policy,*(150), 54-55. Retrieved from ABI/INFORM Global. (Document ID: 888792291).

Kohut, A., & Wike, R. (2008). Assessing globalization: Benefits and drawbacks of trade and integration. *Harvard International Review, 30*(1), 70-74. Retrieved from ABI/INFORM Global. (Document ID: 1504550061).

Nizamuddin, A. (2007). Multinational corporations and economic development: The lessons of Singapore. *International Social Science Review, 82*(3 & 4), 149-162.

Wirth, D. (2009). The international organization for standardization: Private voluntary standards as swords and shields. *Boston College Environmental Affairs Law Review, 36*(1), 79-102. Retrieved from Academic Search Premier. (AN 37181941).

Slide 25